AD 376–82

COMBAT

Late Roman Infantryman VERSUS Gothic Warrior

Murray Dahm

Illustrated by Giuseppe Rava

OSPREY PUBLISHING
Bloomsbury Publishing Plc
Kemp House, Chawley Park, Cumnor Hill, Oxford OX2 9PH, UK
29 Earlsfort Terrace, Dublin 2, Ireland
1385 Broadway, 5th Floor, New York, NY 10018, USA
E-mail: info@ospreypublishing.com
www.ospreypublishing.com

OSPREY is a trademark of Osprey Publishing Ltd

First published in Great Britain in 2021

A catalogue record for this book is available from the British Library.

ISBN: PB 9781472845283; eBook 9781472845290;
ePDF 9781472845269; XML 9781472845276

21 22 23 24 25 10 9 8 7 6 5 4 3 2 1

Maps by www.bounford.com
Index by Rob Munro
Typeset by PDQ Digital Media Solutions, Bungay, UK
Printed and bound in India by Replika Press Private Ltd.

Osprey Publishing supports the Woodland Trust, the UK's leading woodland conservation charity.

To find out more about our authors and books visit **www.ospreypublishing.com**. Here you will find extracts, author interviews, details of forthcoming events and the option to sign up for our newsletter.

Dedication

For Rae, Eloise and Siena.

Author's note

In modern works, the terms 'Visigoths' and 'Ostrogoths' can be found (and even 'Romanians' and 'Bulgarians'). Following the sources cited in this work, I have used the term 'Goths' (and occasionally 'barbarians') even when the ancient authors used different terms which refer to the same peoples. Although variant spellings exist, I have chosen to use the terms 'Greuthungi', 'Theruingi' and 'Halani' throughout this work; these are Ammianus' spellings. The term 'Marcianopolis' has been used to differentiate between that city and Adrianople (rather than using 'Adrianopolis' or 'Marcianople').

Artist's note

Readers may care to note that the original paintings from which the colour plates in this book were prepared are available for private sale. All reproduction copyright whatsoever is retained by the publishers. All enquiries should be addressed to:

info@g-rava.it

The publishers regret that they can enter into no correspondence upon this matter.

CONTENTS

Introduction

In AD 376 an entire nation of the Goths gathered on the northern banks of the Danube River and asked permission to enter and settle within the Roman Empire. Rome had long had contact with the Goths, and with two peoples, the Theruingi and the Greuthungi (probably both confederations), in particular. The Eastern Roman Emperor, Valens (r. 364–78), had fought against both peoples as recently as 366–69, campaigning north of the Danube. During these campaigns large numbers of the Goths may have converted to Christianity to strengthen their ties with Rome. In particular they converted to Arian Christianity, the faith of the emperor Valens, but one at odds with orthodox, Nicene Christianity. This was to have important, far-reaching ramifications. After peace was concluded in 369, more Goths entered the Roman Empire, to settle and serve in its armies in ever-increasing numbers.

What happened in 376, however, was on a scale never witnessed before. Only one (fragmentary) source gives us a number, but Eunapius tells us

The Arch of Constantine in the Forum in Rome combines relief sculpture from earlier periods with 4th-century material. Although the Arch of Constantine was constructed in *c.*315, much of the Roman equipment depicted would have been the same as that used during the wars of the 370s, some 60 years later. The shields (both round and oval), tunics and helmets are contemporary. (VW Pics/ Universal Images Group via Getty Images)

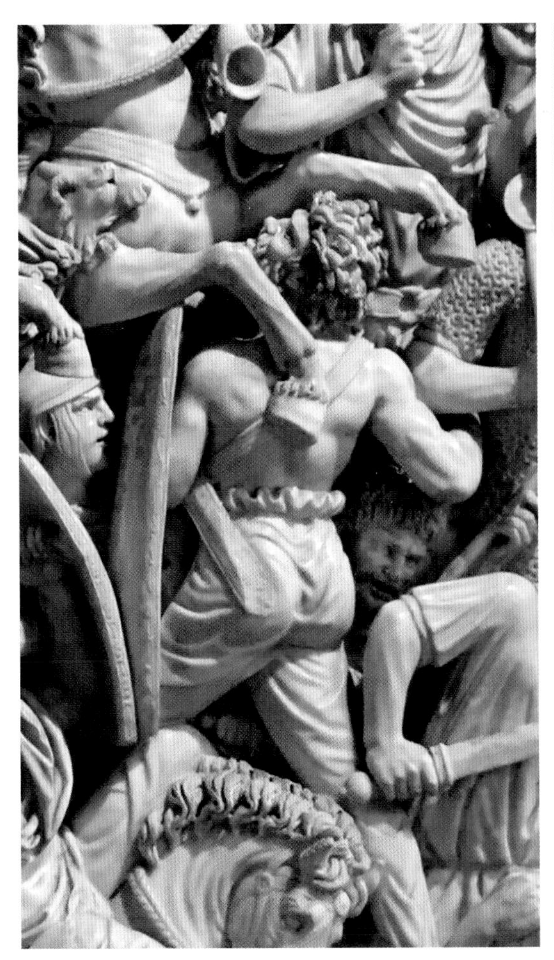

(F42) in his *Historia he meta Dexippon* (*Chronicle after Dexippus*) – known as the *Universal History* – that the initial request to settle in Thrace was made by 200,000 people of the Theruingi under the leadership of Alavivus and Fritigern. They offered to become troops in Roman armies in return. This was an attractive offer to an empire which struggled to find enough new recruits to man its armies. The Greuthungi and other peoples would follow. What forced these groups to the banks of the Danube were devastating advances made by a people 'hitherto unknown' (Zosimus, 20.3): the Huns. The pressure of Hunnic advances in the 370s pushed multiple Gothic groups further south, eventually forcing the Theruingi against the Danube, probably in the spring of 376, desperate to be allowed to cross.

The Gothic request was forwarded to Valens, at that time at Antioch, preparing for a Persian campaign. When permission was granted to enter, the Roman commanders, the *comes* Lupicinus and *dux* Maximus, took advantage, practising extortion on the Goths by charging exorbitant amounts for meagre provisions. (The Goths had probably consumed whatever stores they had brought with them while waiting for permission to enter the empire.) Worse was to come. Marched to Marcianopolis, the capital of Moesia Secunda (Moesia Inferior) in the diocese of Thrace, the Goths were not allowed to enter the city to obtain supplies and began to protest

ABOVE LEFT
No exactly contemporary depictions of Goths survive. This detail from the Ludovisi Sarcophagus, found in 1621 near the Porta Tiburtina in Rome and now in the Museo Nazionale Romano di Palazzo Altemps (Inv. 8547) in Rome, depicts a stereotypical 'barbarian' with unkempt hair and beard, wearing trousers but no armour. (Jastrow/Wikimedia/Public Domain)

ABOVE RIGHT
Another typical 'barbarian' from the Roman perspective. This one wears a cloak held in place by a plate brooch and also a long-sleeved tunic. Note also the hexagonal shield he bears and its grip. (Sailko/Wikimedia/CC BY-SA 3.0)

The Gothic War, AD 376–82

MAP KEY

The most likely places for the Theruingi and Greuthungi Goths to have crossed over into the Roman Empire were along the Danube River in the Roman provinces of Moesia Secunda and Scythia (or Scythia Minor), perhaps at Appiaria (modern-day Ryahovo, Bulgaria), or Durostorum (modern-day Silistra, Bulgaria), or perhaps south-west of these at Sextaginta Prista (on the Danube in modern-day Ruse, Bulgaria). The Goths' destination, Marcianopolis (modern-day Devnya, Bulgaria), the capital city of Moesia Secunda and largest city in the diocese of Thrace, seems to make Durostorum most likely, as there was no direct road from Appiaria to Marcianopolis. Although the Goths subsequently ignored Roman roads on their journeys, the Romans probably moved them along those roads at first in 376. In the emperor Valens' campaigns against the Goths in 366 (Ammianus 27.5.2), he had based himself at Daphne or Constantiana Daphne (either modern-day Grădiştea or Corabia, both in Romania), both sites being between Appiaria and Durostorum. A fourth possible crossing point was at Noviodunum (or Novidunum), near modern-day Isaccea, Romania. This would have meant that they crossed into the province of Scythia (or Scythia Minor) rather than Moesia Secunda, but Marcianopolis may still have been their destination. Noviodunum had been the base for Valens' campaigns against the Greuthungi in 369 (Ammianus, 27.5.6). The march south would have been much longer, however – some 300km – and Tomis (modern-day Constanța, Romania), halfway between the two, might have made a more logical destination. The case for Moesia Secunda seems stronger; and the Greuthungi, who crossed later in 376, probably crossed at Noviodunum.

Once across the Danube, the Romans marched the Theruingi to Marcianopolis, 120km south of the river. The Goths revolted and won a victory just north of the city, then overran territory in Thrace before withdrawing to the Haemus Mountains.

In 377 the Goths faced new Roman armies sent against them at the Willows, a battlefield the location of which was probably in the triangle between Tomis, Durostorum and Marcianopolis. The Goths were then forced back to the Haemus Mountains, but the Romans withdrew, allowing the Goths free rein as far as the Hellespont and the Rhodope Mountains. The Goths fought another Roman force at Dibaltum (near modern-day Debelt, Bulgaria). The year 378 saw the Goths on the rampage once again but they withdrew north or north-east of Adrianople (modern-day Edirne Merkez, Turkey) where Valens met them in battle. After the battle the Goths were unable to take Constantinople (modern-day Istanbul, Turkey) or Perinthus (near modern-day Marmara Ereğlisi, Turkey), and spilled into Macedonia, Thessaly and perhaps even Pannonia.

violently. They had probably surrendered their arms as a provision of entry, but they nevertheless began to fight their Roman guards. Lupicinus invited Alavivus and Fritigern to a banquet at which he planned to assassinate them. Fritigern realized this and either made his escape or persuaded his host that he could calm the rioters. Instead, he rejoined his people, moved away from the city walls, and put out a call for all the Goths to join him. Unarmed or not, the Goths were in open revolt and began to pillage the countryside, taking the supplies they had been denied. Lupicinus and Maximus gathered their forces and moved against the Goths, but they were overwhelmed when the unarmed Goths charged them. Equipping themselves with the weapons and armour of the Romans, the Goths spread out and continued to rampage throughout Thrace.

This first encounter between Gothic warriors and Roman infantrymen highlighted the fact that Roman arms, training and traditions were no match for the untamed ferocity of the Goths. On both sides, the weapons and equipment were largely the same, especially after the Goths equipped themselves with Roman arms and armour. The Goths had the advantage of numbers, but the Romans had many men to call upon and a tradition of discipline and training which should have tipped the balance in their favour. The events of the next 2½ years would show, however, that Rome's armies were no longer capable of withstanding 'barbarian' invasions and the empire was vulnerable to being overrun.

Roman frontier
Diocesan boundary
TAIFALI
CARPATHIAN MOUNTAINS
THERUINGI
Sirmium
PANNONIA
Viminacium
MOESIA SUPERIOR
Morava
Drina
DIOCESE OF ILLYRICUM
DIOCESE OF DACIA
Naissus
Ratiaria
Danube
DACIA RIPENSIS
Noviodunum
SCYTHIA
Tomis
Appiaria
Durostorum
Sextaginta Prista
MOESIA SECUNDA
Nicopolis
Marcianopolis
DIOCESE OF THRACE
HAEMUS MOUNTAINS
PRAEVALITANA
DARDANIA
DACIA MEDITERRANEA
Serdica
Doclea
Tonzos
Cabyle
Beroe
THRACIA
Dibaltum
Black Sea
Philippopolis
Hebrus
HAEMIMONTUS
Scupi
RHODOPE MOUNTAINS
Stobi
Strymon
Nestos
RHODOPE
Adrianople
Nice in Thrace
Axios
MACEDONIA SECUNDA
MACEDONIA PRIMA
EUROPA
Constantinople
Perinthus
Thessalonica
Beroea
DIOCESE OF MACEDONIA
Hellespont
DIOCESE OF ASIANA
DIOCESE OF PONTICA
Aegean Sea
EPIRUS VETUS
THESSALIA
N
0
100 miles
0
100km

The Opposing Sides

ORIGINS AND FORCE STRUCTURE

Roman

The Late Roman Army was very different from that of the 1st and 2nd centuries. In the reign of Diocletian (r. 284–305), a huge number of reforms were undertaken, and several more phases of reform followed during the 4th century. The most important of these for the wars against the Goths was the splitting of the empire into East and West. Although subsequent emperors fought to reunify the empire, when Valentinian I (r. 364–75) became emperor, he reinstituted the spilt and made his brother Valens the Eastern Roman Emperor.

Essentially, the armies now revolved around *limitanei* (sing. *limitaneus*), the troops who manned the borders of the empire and who were stationed in a particular border province. Thus we have the *limitanei* of Moesia Secunda and Scythia taking part in the battles of 376–78. The men in these armies were resident in particular towns and their positions became hereditary. There were also more mobile forces called *comitatenses* (sing. *comitatus*). Both these types of army included units termed *legiones* (sing. *legio*, legion), *auxilia* (sing. *auxilium*, an auxiliary force) and cavalry *vexillationes* (sing. *vexillatio*, a detachment from a *legio* or the *auxilia*), although they were of different strengths. The *vexillationes* in *limitanei* armies could also be called *alae* (sing. *ala*, 'wing') or *cunei* (sing. *cuneus*, 'wedge').

The most important sources for these matters are the histories of Ammianus Marcellinus and the *Notitia Dignitatum* (*List of Offices*), which post-dates the battles being examined. We must rely on these sources (and others) because the period saw a decrease in inscriptions and military tombstone burials. There are a plethora of unit names in the *Notitia Dignitatum* and in some cases a unit in the East shares the same name as a unit in the West, sometimes with the terms *iuniores* (juniors) or *seniores* (seniors) used to differentiate them; usually, *seniores* were in the West and *iuniores* in the East, though not always. These units were also a mix of infantry and some cavalry units. Some units' titles (such as *sagittarii*, 'archers') continued to carry a meaning relevant to their troop type. Other units' titles, such as the *lanciarii* (light cavalry equipped with lances) and *mattiarii* (possibly named after their weapon, the *mattium*, of which nothing is known) at the battle of Adrianople (Ammianus, 31.13.8) or the *Cornuti* (meaning 'horned', a reference to their helmets) at the battle of Dibaltum (Ammianus, 31.8.9), may have ceased to differentiate them as troop types by the late 4th century. Thus the *legiones* known as the *Ioviani* and *Herculiani*, formed under Diocletian as guard units, lost their guard status but retained their titles as *legiones*. At the same time there were units whose titles did continue to refer to their battlefield role, such as the *peditibus sagittariis* ('infantry archers') in 378 (Ammianus, 31.12.2). There were also units of *exculcatores* (javelinmen) and *funditores* (slingers).

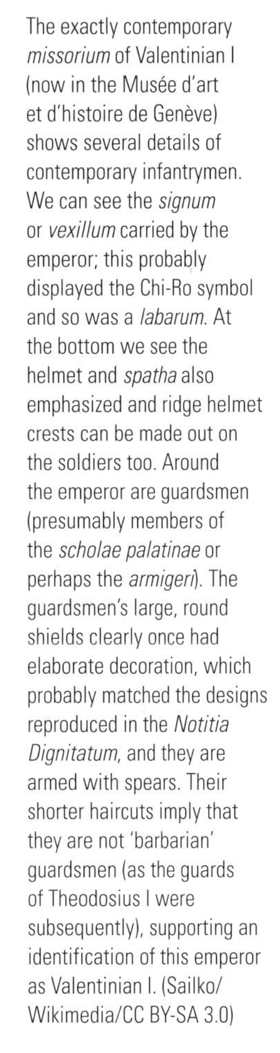

The exactly contemporary *missorium* of Valentinian I (now in the Musée d'art et d'histoire de Genève) shows several details of contemporary infantrymen. We can see the *signum* or *vexillum* carried by the emperor; this probably displayed the Chi-Ro symbol and so was a *labarum*. At the bottom we see the helmet and *spatha* also emphasized and ridge helmet crests can be made out on the soldiers too. Around the emperor are guardsmen (presumably members of the *scholae palatinae* or perhaps the *armigeri*). The guardsmen's large, round shields clearly once had elaborate decoration, which probably matched the designs reproduced in the *Notitia Dignitatum*, and they are armed with spears. Their shorter haircuts imply that they are not 'barbarian' guardsmen (as the guards of Theodosius I were subsequently), supporting an identification of this emperor as Valentinian I. (Sailko/ Wikimedia/CC BY-SA 3.0)

The mobile field armies had no fixed base, but were usually based in a particular area, such as at Marcianopolis (modern-day Devnya, Bulgaria). In such cases they were probably billeted in the area and may have taken time to assemble (Ammianus, 31.5.9). The emperor himself usually commanded one of the *comitatenses*, in which case it became the *comitatus praesentalis*, the 'army in the emperor's presence'. Units with this army would become *palatini* ('palace troops'), a title of status because they were in the emperor's army (so *auxilia palatini*, for instance). In addition to the *comitatus praesentalis*, the emperor also had elite guard units known collectively as *scholae* (sing. *schola*); these imperial escort cavalry units replaced the Praetorian Guard, which had been disbanded by Constantine I (r. 306–37) in 312. There were seven units in the Eastern *scholae*, each of an approximate strength of 500 men. Therefore, the men of the *scutarii*, heavy infantry or cavalry who originally used *scuta* (sing. *scutum*, a large rectangular shield), and *sagittarii* at the battle of Adrianople (Ammianus, 31.12.16) may actually have represented 1,000 or 1,500 cavalry (assuming that *scutarii* referred to both units in the *scholae*). We might assume that the left wing of cavalry which did not make it to the field at Adrianople may also have contained *scholae* regiments and so another 1,000–1,500 men. Dressed in white tunics, 40 of the most trusted *scholae palatinae* would form the *candidati*, the personal bodyguard of the emperor. Also among the guard units were the *protectores*, infantrymen organized into an *auxilium*, and the *protectores domestici* (the emperor's personal guard in which Ammianus served), a *vexillatio*. These were commanded by the *comes domesticorum equitum* (commander of the cavalry of the emperor's personal guard) and *comes domesticorum peditum* (commander of the household troops of the emperor's personal guard) under the *comes domesticorum*; they were often used for special assignments, such as those undertaken by Richomeres, the Western *comes domesticorum*, in 377 and 378. *Protectores* could also serve as junior officers.

Ammianus tells us (31.5.10) not to expect exact numbers of casualties in his account of the Gothic Wars and this deliberate lack of numbers means that we are often left struggling to estimate the sizes of the forces involved. It possibly indicates that there was no standard unit size at the time, or that Ammianus simply expected his readers to understand how many men were

1

2

3

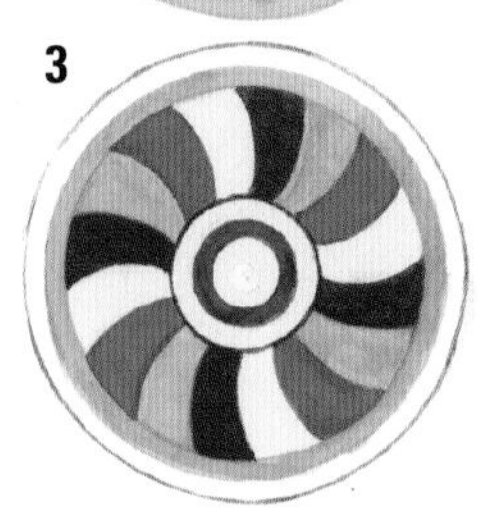

4

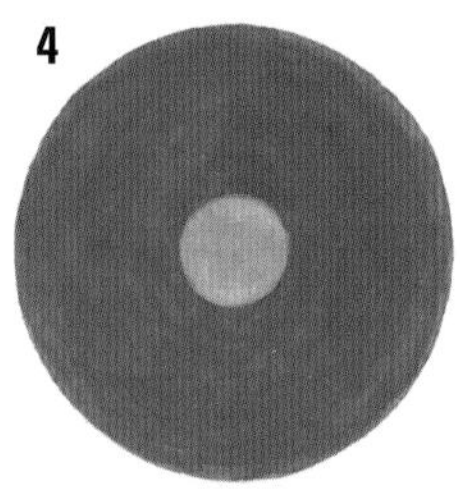

5

These shield designs, taken from the *Notitia Dignitatum*, include those attributed to the *Equites armigeri seniores* (**1**), the infantry under the command of the *Comes domesticorum* (**2**), the *Constantini Dafnenses* (**3**), the *Lanciarii Stobenses* (**4**) and the *Batavi iuniores* (**5**).

in each army and unit. Where we can tell, however, these numbers varied, indicating that there was no standard unit size, especially not in practice.

Estimates of the size of the Late Roman Army are usually divided into 'large' and 'small' camps. For the Roman forces at the battle of Adrianople, for which we have abundant evidence, some have estimated their strength at 15,000–20,000 troops. The Gothic forces are given a strength of 10,000 – the one number Ammianus mentions (31.12.3) – although it seems clear that this number was not intended to represent the whole body of the Goths. Higher estimates for the number of Roman troops present at Adrianople stretch to 30,000–40,000, and even to 60,000. These higher estimates are usually rejected by modern historians. It should be noted, however, that Ammianus records (31.13.18) a high tally of officers who fell, which supports a higher estimate rather than a lower one. Ammianus' mention of 35 *tribuni* (sing. *tribunus*) who lost their lives in the battle certainly implies the presence of a large number of units (although those 35 are mentioned as having no particular command), which would be difficult to accommodate in a smaller force. A *tribunus* was a specific command rank in the *scholae*, *comitatenses* and *limitanei*; a *tribunus* commanded a *legio*, but the term could also be used to denote the commander of any unit. Ammianus adds other *numeri* (detachments), all of which suggest a larger rather than a smaller force. *Numeri* may have numbered 300 men each (based on Ammianus, 20.4.2) and there were multiple such units at Adrianople.

We can posit that the Roman commander Sebastianus' army before Adrianople included seven *legiones* (Ammianus, 31.11.2; Zosimus, 4.23.2) and add to it units from Valens' *comitatus praesentalis*, plus units brought by Richomeres and others. The *comitatus praesentalis* which accompanied Valens may have numbered between 20,000 and 30,000 men. In his account of the battle, Ammianus mentions by name seven units: the *sagittarii*, *scutarii*, *lanciarii*, *mattiarii*, *armigeri*, *Batavi* and *candidati*. Two of these were *scholae* units, and two bodyguard units. Several of the others may have been *auxilia* or *auxilia palatini* units. MacDowall mentions (2001: 23) the pairing of *auxilia* units, perhaps suggesting that infantry took the field in units of 1,000 men – the *lanciarii* and *mattiarii* are paired by Ammianus (31.13.8). All of this tends to suggest a higher number. Others have estimated *limitanei legiones*' strength at only 500 men each and cavalry units at 300, but some cavalry units had an actual strength of only 80–160 men.

What is more, the comparison made by Ammianus to Rome's disaster at the battle of Cannae in 216 BC (31.13.19), where the Romans lost between 40,000 and 70,000 men, cannot have been too wide of the mark. Ammianus states (31.13.18) that barely one-third of the Roman participants survived the battle of Adrianople, and (taking the lowest estimate of the casualties at Cannae) an army of 60,000 at Adrianople of which 20,000 survived fits with these estimates. Themistius claimed (*Oration 16:* 206d) that 'armies' entirely disappeared like shadows, implying that the loss – and the numbers of Roman troops involved – was a significant one.

By the time of the *Notitia Dignitatum* in *c.*390 the Eastern Roman Empire's armies consisted of approximately 104,000 men in the *comitatenses*, 3,500 in the *scholae* units and 195,000 troops in the *limitanei*. The *Magister Militum per Thracias* could call upon approximately 27,000 men based at

Marcianopolis, while the *dux* (a commander of troops) of Moesia Secunda could call upon 7,000 of the province's *limitanei* (Scythia had an additional 8,000 men). There were two armies termed *palatini praesentalis* (the emperor's palace troops), both based at Constantinople and each consisting of 22,000–23,000 men; the split into two armies was probably made after the battle of Adrianople, so we may combine them into one *praesentalis* army in 378. Assuming that the *limitanei* of Scythia and Illyricum – an additional 31,000 men – were not called upon, and the armies further east (60,000) and in Egypt (28,000) were also not involved, this leaves an army of 82,500 men. Some units guarded Adrianople, some cavalry never made it to the battle; thus, taking into account other absences, we can estimate an army of 60,000 men at Adrianople without unreasonable exaggeration (and from which 40,000 would be lost, as at Cannae). These numbers are based on *comitatus legiones* fielding 1,000 men each, *vexillationes* and *auxilia* numbering 500 men each, *limitanei legiones* fielding 500 men each and other units mustering 250 men each. Even these numbers may be too low, however; otherwise the defeat at Adrianople would have deprived Thrace and the area around Constantinople of most of their troops. Given how quickly the emperor Theodosius I (r. 379–95) tried to recruit a new army after the battle of Adrianople and then settled with the Goths when this effort failed, however, the idea of a Thrace stripped of Roman troops may not be too far from the truth.

The *Notitia Dignitatum* contains details of units formed – and divisions made – after Adrianople, but records that each of the *praesentalis* armies contained 12 cavalry units and 24 infantry units, so perhaps a single army had double these numbers before 378. The army in Thrace had seven cavalry units and 21 infantry units. Therefore there was a mixture of cavalry and infantry units, although infantry dominated. In the sources for the Gothic Wars we are not told of units except in the vaguest terms. For example, in the *comitatus* of Thrace we find that less than 15 per cent of the army was cavalry, and that the *praesentalis* armies each had just under 30 per cent cavalry. The status of units may also have come into play. Often considered inferior or soft, units of the *limitanei* were the lowest-status troops. *Comitatus* units ranked higher and *palatini* above them. The pinnacle of a soldier's status in the late 4th century was to serve in a *scholae* unit. In the wars against the Goths, however, the troops of the *limitanei* fared no worse than their more senior colleagues, so it is difficult to make a qualitative distinction. Indeed, several units which may have belonged to the *limitanei* appear to have conducted themselves just as well as their higher-status colleagues.

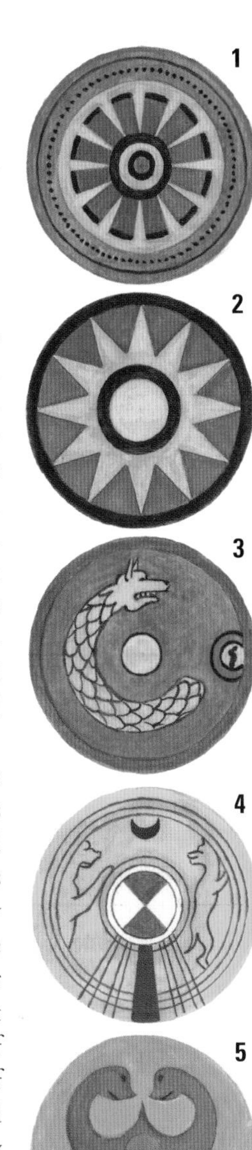

Also drawn from the *Notitia Dignitatum*, these shield designs include those associated with the *Lanciarii seniores* (**1**), the *Schola scutatorium prima* (**2**), the *Schola scutatorium secunda* (**3**), the *Mattiarii seniores* (**4**) and the *Cornuti seniores* (**5**).

The strength of late-4th-century Roman Army units is difficult to assess and, unlike the period up to the end of the 2nd century, little information is available. It is also unlikely that units across the empire each fielded the same number of men, making it even harder to estimate the numbers of troops involved. Ammianus records (18.9.3–4 & 19.2.14) that seven *legiones*, amounting to 20,000 men, were crammed into the city of Amida (modern-day Diyarbakir, Turkey) in 359. Even though Ammianus admits there were civilian men and other soldiers (19.2.14) at Amida, the *legiones* were clearly stronger than the 1,000 men per *legio* figure that is usually assumed. *Legiones* and *auxilia* were the two main types of infantry unit in all Late Roman armies. Each *legio* is usually estimated at 1,000 men; some were divided into cohorts,

COMBAT Roman infantryman

This young Late Roman infantryman from the *Divitenses Gallicani* of the *comitatus* of Thrace faces the Gothic forces in revolt outside Marcianopolis in 376. His expression is one of surprise, as he is unexpectedly about to receive the charge of an enemy he thought was cowed. His left leg is forward with his weight behind his shield, ready to receive the Gothic onslaught.

Marcianopolis, AD 376

Weapons, dress and equipment

His *hasta* (**1**) is held in a low defensive position; it has a triangular iron blade (**2**). On his left hip he wears a *spatha* (**3**) in a scabbard suspended from a baldric in combination with his military belt.

He wears a two-part silvered Roman ridge helm (**4**) with a typical horsehair crest (**5**). A rear flap on the helmet protects the back of the neck, but the cheek pieces are loose as he has had to prepare for combat in a rush. He also has not had time to put on his greaves. He wears bronze *lorica squamata* (scale armour), consisting of a tunic (**6**) and collar (**7**) over a decorated long-sleeved tunic and leggings (**8**). He wears puttees and typical Roman shoes of the period (**9**).

He stands with his shield (**10**) pushed forward; it is painted with the design of his unit with a central boss. The handle for the shield is an off-centre grip on its inner surface.

each with perhaps 500 men. These are paper strengths, however, and, in the field, numbers could be much smaller; an Egyptian papyrus records a cohort with only 164 men.

Writing in the 6th century, Agathias estimates (5.13.7–8) that the Roman Army in the 'old days' numbered 645,000 men; this is assumed to be a reference to the reign of Constantine I. Zosimus wrote (2.15.1–2 & 2.22.1–2) that the Roman Army numbered 581,000 men in total during the first quarter of the 4th century. Although some modern commentators argue that numbers remained consistently high until the late 4th century, other scholars posit that the troop levels cited by the ancient authors are paper numbers which do not reflect the realities of units in the field; accordingly, these commentators revise the total number down to 400,000 or thereabouts. In the battles examined in this study, I have argued for the higher estimates of troops involved on both sides.

Gothic

The very identity of the Gothic groups which crossed the Danube in 376 is problematic: Eunapius and Zosimus refer to them as Scyths, while Ammianus calls them Goths of various groups – especially the Theruingi and Greuthungi, although Halani (or Alans) and Huns are mixed in, and the Taifali. Other ancient peoples are also included in Gothic pre-history. The Goths seem

The *missorium* of Theodosius I was found in Almendralejo, Spain, in 1847, and is now in the Real Academia de Bellas Artes de San Fernando in Madrid. This is another exactly contemporary depiction of Roman infantrymen; we can see shield designs and spears carried by several Gothic soldiers in the emperor's service. We can tell they are Gothic by their long hair and neck rings; the soldiers on the *missorium* of Valentinian I may also be Gothic, but the details are more difficult to discern. (DEA PICTURE LIBRARY/Getty Images)

likely to have been the Černjachov or Sîntana-de-Mureş Culture, which spread over large sections of modern eastern Europe (Ukraine, Romania, Moldova and Belarus); others have been suggested, such as the Wielbark Culture, but this was located closer to the Baltic Sea and was slightly earlier. Earlier peoples, such as the Gutones of the 1st and 2nd centuries, lived on the Vistula River and had been part of the Wielbark Culture. Jordanes claimed (*Getica* 25) that the Goths originated in Scandinavia and until the 19th century this claim was accepted without question; indeed, early archaeologists sought to prove Jordanes' account. As scientific archaeology developed, however, Jordanes' interpretation came to be questioned. From 1945 onwards theories changed and archaeology since has uncovered much that is new, although controversies of identification remain.

This detail of the *missorium* of Theodosius I shows more clearly the details of the shields, armour and arms of the Gothic soldiers next to a seated Arcadius. The neck rings are a further indication of the soldiers' 'barbarian' origins. The *missorium* was made in 388 to commemorate the tenth anniversary of the reign of Theodosius I, by which time Gothic soldiers had been even further absorbed into the Roman military system. One wears *lorica squamata* (scale armour), while the other seems to wear a highly decorated *sagum* (cloak). The shoes match surviving leather examples. (Werner Forman/ Universal Images Group/Getty Images)

The use of 'cultures' as a term to delineate these peoples is more recent, although each culture could have many 'peoples'. Thus the Goths might be a single culture, but could contain the Theruingi, the Greuthungi and also the Taifali (Ammianus, 31.9.3) and be allied to other people such as the Halani (Ammianus, 31.3–4). There are 12 groups of Goths mentioned in Ammianus, five of which became what we know as the Visigoths and Ostrogoths, so the picture is complicated.

The Romans were entirely familiar with the Goths; there had been Gothic invasions in the 3rd century and Gothic campaigns conducted by Valens as recently as the 360s, after which he made peace with the Theruingi and the Greuthungi. Groups of Goths had already settled within the empire and had spread as far as Pontus; their men already supplied recruits for Roman armies both in the West and the East (Ammianus, 31.6.1–3 & 31.16.8). Several of our sources (Sozomen, 6.37; Socrates, 4.34; Vegetius, 1.2) criticize Valens for allowing the recruitment and training of Roman recruits to slacken. If anything, this was a longstanding trend and not one which should be solely attributed to Valens; but his expectation of being able to rely on the Goths as a recruitment pool certainly did nothing to allay or reverse such a trend.

A Roman army of 60,000 men would not have hesitated to attack 'only' 10,000 Goths at Adrianople, even though the Goths were on high ground and had the protecting rampart of their wagon laager (Ammianus, 31.12.16). There must have been greater numbers of Goths than this. A fragment of Eunapius' *Universal History* (F42), one which Zosimus did not excerpt in his *New History*, tells us that there were 200,000 'Scyths' – the only firm figure

Gothic warrior

This Gothic warrior has armed himself with Roman equipment. He is emaciated from starvation and his hair and beard are unkempt; his expression is one of desperate determination. He charges the Roman forces outside Marcianopolis without any sense of unit cohesion and his actions are more about a personal act of bravery for his chief.

Marcianopolis, AD 376

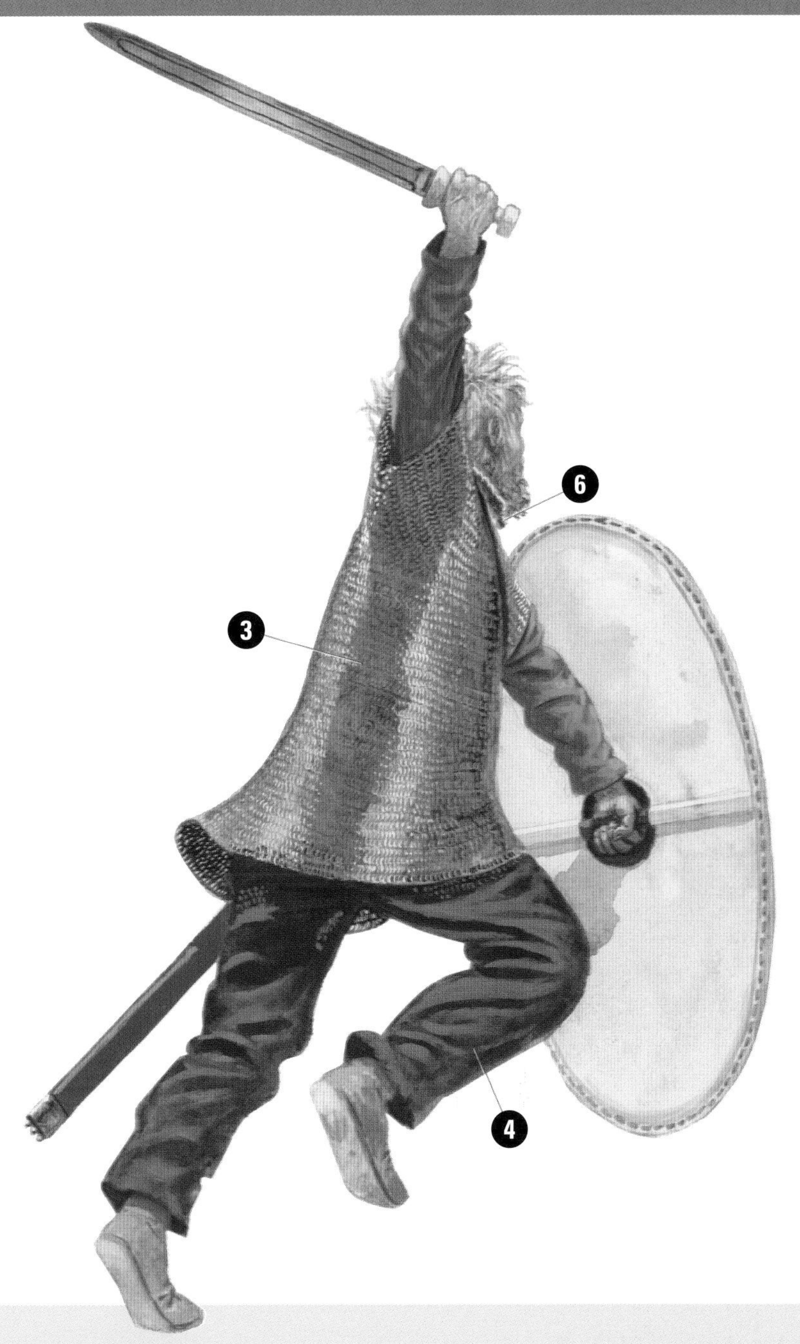

Weapons, dress and equipment

Crossing into the Roman Empire without his weapons, our warrior has armed himself with a Roman *spatha* (**1**) which he wields over his head; its scabbard (**2**) is worn on a baldric over his shoulder. He wears a loose-fitting Roman mail tunic (**3**) taken from a Roman soldier, and characteristically 'barbarian' trousers (**4**) with boots (**5**). He wears a gold torc around his neck (**6**).

He has taken his shield (**7**) from a Roman guard charged with escorting the Goths to Marcianopolis, a member of one of the units of the *limitanei* of Moesia Secunda commanded by the *dux* Maximus who had treated the Goths so poorly. Our warrior brandishes his newly acquired shield in a non-defensive position as he makes his reckless charge. (The shield designs of the units of the *limitanei* of Moesia Secunda are not recorded in the *Notitia Dignitatum*, but the design depicted here is modelled on contemporary patterns.)

for them in the sources – gathered on the riverbank in 376 and begging to cross; the river is not named, but we should assume it to be the Danube. Some modern estimates take the 200,000 figure as the entire population and Eunapius' 'men fit for war' (F42) would account for between one-fifth and one-quarter of that population, so between 40,000 and 50,000 men. The figure could be higher: the Halani are described by Ammianus (31.2.22) as having all the men as warriors, so perhaps one-third would have fought.

It should be remembered, however, that Eunapius' 200,000 figure referred only to those who crossed initially in 376. After that (and in time for the battles of 377 and 378), whole other nations of Goths had crossed – the Greuthungi, the Halani and the Taifali – not to mention various groups of allied Huns. If the Greuthungi numbered approximately the same as the Theruingi, then we have an approximate population of 400,000 Goths and a warrior population of 80,000, plus Taifali, Halani and Hun cavalry. A later fragment of Eunapius' account (F48.2) states that countless groups of Goths crossed into the empire and more followed simply because there was no one to prevent them. This suggests that the numbers of the Goths may indeed have been very high, especially in 377 and 378. The presence at the battle of Adrianople of a very large number of Goths – most of whom were concealed, and including the cavalry, who were absent at the opening of the battle – is not unthinkable, and fits with Ammianus' account (31.13.3) of hordes of Goths appearing unexpectedly. Subsequent accounts which suggest that well-trained Roman legionaries could defeat larger numbers of Goths (for example, Vegetius, 1.1) imply that the Romans always expected their troops to be outnumbered by their Gothic opponents, but that with the benefit of superior discipline and training, the Romans could still prevail, as they nearly always had.

The motivation of the Goths during 376–78 is obvious from Ammianus' account. They were starved and mistreated, and when this prompted an open revolt outside Marcianopolis in 376, the Romans were surprised and overwhelmed. The Romans continued to be surprised at the ferocity of the Goths; even unarmed they pressed their attack and defeated well-armed and -armoured enemies. Ammianus suggests (31.5.14) that Roman armies had become soft, but it was only a few years since the Roman victories of the late 360s. Despite the fact that the emperor's troops had prevailed over the Goths in previous battles, the desperate determination now exhibited by the Goths enabled them to defeat the Romans.

According with the accounts of Zosimus (20.4.5) and Ammianus (31.4.4), Eunapius (F42) notes that the Goths promised they would provide reinforcements for the Roman armies. Word was sent to Valens at Antioch and debate among the Romans ensued. The precise nature of the debate is related differently by Eunapius and Ammianus. Eunapius records (F42) that Valens admitted the 'barbarians' out of chagrin that the emperors Gratian (r. 367–83) and Valentinian II (r. 375–92) had divided the Western Roman Empire without consulting him, but also because Roman forces might be substantially increased as a result. First, however, the Goths had to surrender their weapons and their children were to be taken as hostages. (These conditions are missing from Ammianus.) Eunapius does not name the corrupt Roman officials Lupicinus and Maximus as Ammianus does (31.4.9), but he does record their misdemeanours – choosing slaves and wives and the healthiest men for their own estates. To ensure this pick of the crop would be theirs, they allowed some Goths to cross while bearing arms.

Orosius relates (7.33.9) that churches were hacked apart by Valens as part of the schism between Nicene and Arian Christianity and has him accepting the Goths into the empire without any treaty (7.33.10) and without handing over their arms. Orosius does not name Lupicinus, but makes reference to the extraordinary greed of the *dux* Maximus, and the hunger and insults inflicted on the Goths that provoked them to rise up in arms. Another Eunapius fragment (F45.3), from the 10th-century Byzantine encyclopedia, the *Suda* (Π 2351), records that Valens received the Goths into the empire in the expectation that they would provide a bulwark against the Huns. Eunapius reveals (F42) his bias against non-Romans, however, by stating that the Goths broke their oaths – Zosimus (4.20.7) has them break their oaths as soon as they set foot in Roman territory – whereas the Roman misdemeanours recorded by Ammianus make the Goths' oath-breaking far more explicable. In Eunapius' account there is the suggestion that the 'barbarians' were threatening to take over the empire with their unexpected revolt, their great numbers causing panic among the Romans. The ensuing depopulation of the area was still evident when Eunapius wrote, leading some to argue that Eunapius' account was written *c.*380, very soon after the battle of Adrianople.

The Church histories (Sozomen, 6.37; Socrates, 4.35) also dwell on the Goths breaking their oaths, but they do not record the atrocities carried out against them. Most then move straight on to the battle of Adrianople with perhaps just a brief sentence on the Goths overrunning Thrace and other territories.

ORGANIZATION AND COMMAND

Roman

We have seen already in the composition of the Late Roman Army how command devolved from the authority of the emperor. Valens had spent much of his reign on campaign, first against the Goths, then preparing for a campaign against the Persians, and then against the Goths again. During the

The Great Hunt mosaic in Villa Romana del Casale, Piazza Armerina in Sicily, is useful for all kinds of details of dress and technology. The wide variety of decoration evident on tunics and cloaks probably allowed individuality within military units; their shields would have identified them, but there is little evidence of mandated colours of tunics or cloaks. That said, two of the slaves on the left of this image appear to share a livery – a red tunic with vertical blue stripes. (Anonymous/Wikimedia/Public Domain)

period 376–78, Valens was initially based at Antioch in Syria with the *comitatus praesentalis*, preparing for a Persian campaign. The emperor could also appoint a *magister militum* ('master of soldiers'), a *magister equitum* ('master of cavalry' or 'master of horse') and a *magister peditum* ('master of infantry' or 'master of foot'). Despite the title, a *magister peditum* or *magister equitum* could also be appointed to command other *comitatus* armies. Usually, however, the other *comitatus* armies were based in a diocese and commanded by a *comes*, the senior military official of a diocese. Thus we find that Lupicinus, the *comes per Thracias*, commanded his own *comitatus* (with additional units probably from the *limitanei* of Moesia Secunda commanded by their *dux*, Maximus) at the battle of Marcianopolis in 376. In 377, Traianus, the *magister peditum*, was appointed to command what were probably the remnants of the same army and sent to Thrace with Profuturus (whose rank we do not know, perhaps *dux* to replace Maximus) with *legiones* from Armenia (Ammianus, 31.7.2). This army was the same size as that of Moesia Secunda. Saturninus, the (temporary) *magister equitum*, then joined them after the battle of the Willows in 377. Units could be transferred around, however, even between Eastern and Western empires. Thus we find Richomeres taking troops under his command to the East in 377 in addition to Frigiderius, the *comes* of Illyricum, taking units from his *comitatus*.

Unlike in earlier periods of Roman military history, we lose sight of the lower ranks in Roman armies of the 4th century. Under the *tribunus* who commanded the *legio*, we find a *primicerius*, his second-in-command. Below him, the *legio* was organized into six *ordines* (sing. *ordo*, a unit of men), each of which included two centuries (theoretically 100 men each). Each *ordo* of 200 men was commanded by a *ducenarius* (sometimes called a senator, although nothing to do with the senatorial class). Second-in-command in the century (below the centurion) was the *biarchus*; below him, a *semissalis* commanded ten men. Units of the *auxilia* seem to have had only three *ordines*, each with two centuries. *Legiones* of the *limitanei* may have been organized as cohorts, with a *tribunus* and six centuries, each commanded by an *ordinarius* (so not divided into two-century *ordines*). Below him was a *biarchus* as in the *legiones* of the *comitatenses*.

Gothic

We have no such information for the Goths. The ancient authors provide some information about bands roving around independently, such as Farnobius with his men and the Taifali (Ammianus, 31.9.4), and of the commanders Alatheus and Saphrax operating under Fritigern and independently (Ammianus, 31.4.12, 31.12.12 & 31.12.17; Jordanes, 140; Zosimus, 4.34.2). We do not know of any further divisions of troops or command, but clearly the Goths had several troop types and independent commands. Given their familiarity with the Roman system, we might argue for similar organization, but nothing in the sources suggests it. The Theruingi had become Romanized during the 4th century through contact with the empire; Ammianus refers (27.5.1) to the long peace and friendship they had enjoyed with Rome in 366, facilitated by trade and employment in the Roman Army. The Theruingi had also been converted to Arian Christianity by the Gothic missionary Wulfila earlier in the century, but none of this tells us that they had adopted Roman military organization.

The activities of Fritigern and the sequence of events leading up to the battle of Adrianople give the lie to the common phrase 'winners write history'; despite the Gothic victories and the permanent establishment of the Gothic peoples within the empire, their version of events does not survive. All of the surviving accounts are Roman (whether written in Latin or Greek), and they sometimes give a very confused picture, which has influenced our view. Even in terms of archaeology there is little to work with, although this situation is improving. We have the Latinization of the names of peoples and individuals which, in many cases are inconsistent; Ammianus names the child-king of the Greuthungi as both Vithericus (31.4.12) and Viderichus (31.3.3).

Unearthed in 1837 and now in the Muzeul National de Istorie a Romaniei in Bucharest, the Pietroasele treasure reveals the highest standards of Gothic art in the late 4th century. This repoussé gold *patera* (bowl) reveals details of Gothic dress and culture, but also the extent of classicizing influence. Pietroasele in Romania was the site of one of Constantine I's forts on the northern bank of the Danube in the late 320s. (DEA/G. DAGLI ORTI/De Agostini via Getty Images)

Beyond the main group level, we are given no insights into Gothic organization, either as sub-groups or in a tactical sense. In Ammianus we find the Theruingi (in several factions), the Greuthungi and also the Halani, the Taifali and some allied Huns. We find mention of the Gothic leaders: Fritigern, Alavivus and Athanaric for the Theruingi – although Ammianus (31.4.13) also associates Athanaric with the Greuthungi; the commanders Alatheus and Saphrax, notionally subordinate to their child-king Vithericus, but in reality exercising command in their own right (Ammianus, 31.4.12), for the Greuthungi; and Farnobius and the Taifali. Ammianus also mentions (31.6.1–3) Sueridus and Colias, the chieftains of Goths (which grouping is not specified) already settled in the empire.

We get no insight into Gothic organization or tactics (other than a ferocious charge) and to understand them it is necessary to read between

This mosaic fragment, held in the Büyük Saray Mozaik Müzesi (Great Palace Mosaic Museum) in Istanbul, Turkey, shows a 'barbarian' portrait. No known portrait of Fritigern exists, but here we see a 'barbarian' depicted as part of a mosaic's border; we can tell he is a 'barbarian' because of his moustache. This mosaic may date from the 5th century, showing the continuity of depictions of 'barbarians' and their customs. (PHAS/Universal Images Group via Getty Images)

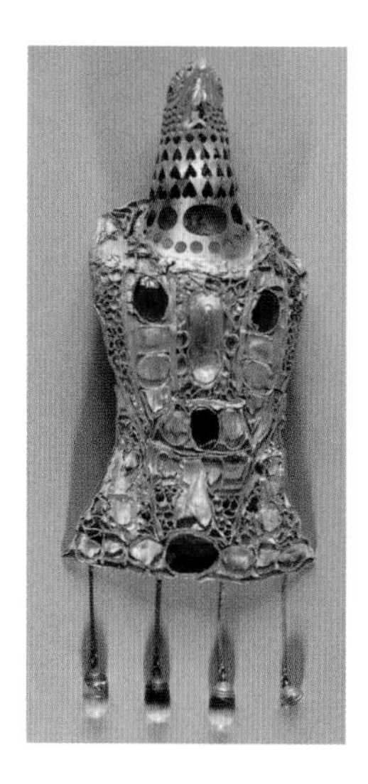

Found in Pietroasele and now in the Muzeul National de Istorie a Romaniei in Bucharest, this gold eagle buckle from the Pietroasele treasure shows the level of splendour and decoration some Goths must have added to their clothing. Originally there were 22 pieces, but now there are only 12; the eagle features on several of them. The quality of the finds led early commentators to assume that the treasure must have belonged to a chieftain. (DEA/G. DAGLI ORTI/De Agostini via Getty Images)

the lines somewhat. Although charges were an important Gothic tactic, they also shot arrows into Roman formations, hurled javelins and clubs, and used swords and axes. Vegetius (1.20) recognized that the archery of the Goths, the Halani and the Huns had taught the Romans a thing or two. There must have been unit organizations (perhaps even with specific battlefield roles), but we remain ignorant of them.

In the Gothic cavalry, too, we find archers and javelinmen. There must have been heavy cavalry as well, as suggested by later archaeology; such troops must have been present to defeat heavy Roman *cataphractarii* (heavily armoured cavalry armed with lances) and *clibanarii* (likewise heavily armoured cavalry, but armed with clubs and axes for close-quarters battle). The Halani may have been heavy cavalry who fought like the Sarmatians depicted on Trajan's Column, although they also used horse-archers. The sources emphasize the charge, but at the battle of Adrianople the Gothic cavalry seem to have surrounded the Roman infantry and continued to shoot missiles into the ranks too. We do get detail on the Hunnic cavalry (Ammianus, 31.2.8–9) who entered battle in wedge-shaped formations and then divided suddenly and attacked rapidly, shooting missiles – arrows and javelins – as well as using nooses plaited from cloth. These nooses were perhaps used as lassos. Ammianus (31.2.21–22) describes the Halani as being similar to the Huns, growing up in the saddle: all men of these cultures were warriors and they delighted in danger and war. This we might apply to Gothic cavalry more generally, although they may have had different fighting styles as demonstrated by the Halani, who were both heavy cavalry and missile cavalry. Zosimus mentions (4.20.4) Hunnic tactics – wheeling, charging, retreating in good time and shooting from their horses – which might have been employed by Gothic cavalry in general.

The limitations of the sources mean that it is difficult to assess the precise nature of Fritigern's leadership; perhaps describing him as the head of a confederation of peoples is the best estimation. In Ammianus' account (31.3.8), we first meet Fritigern as one of the leaders of the Theruingi as they crossed the Danube in 376. In Socrates and Sozomen he is introduced earlier, but their picture does little to clarify his position. Fritigern does seem to have wrested control of the Theruingi from Athanaric in a conflict that continued into the 380s. Jordanes (135, 142) calls him chief and king, so he may have held kingly status; Ammianus also calls him king, both alongside Alavivus (31.5.7) and on his own (31.6.5). According to Zosimus (4.36), Fritigern continued as leader of the Theruingi, but was still warring with rivals.

TACTICS AND EQUIPMENT

Roman and Gothic equipment was largely very similar throughout the period of the Gothic Wars, especially after the Goths armed themselves with captured Roman gear. Both armies used the long sword known as the *spatha*, although Ammianus uses the terms *murco* (31.7.12, 31.7.14 & 31.13.2), *ferrum* (31.15.1) and *gladius* (31.2.23, 31.5.9, 31.7.13 & 31.13.5), all of which mean 'sword' (the term *gladius* does not refer to the distinctive short Roman sword, however, which had fallen out of use in the 2nd century).

Built in the early 4th century, the Arch of Galerius in Thessaloniki, Greece, shows a remarkable range of military equipment. Here we see soldiers in scale armour wearing *spangenhelm* or ridge helmets and with unit *vexilla* or *signa* behind. The *signum* remained in use after the triumph of Christianity in 337, becoming the *labarum*, which displayed the Chi Rho symbol. The Arch, which commemorates Galerius' victory over the Persians in 298, is useful for its depiction of those military items that continued in use through to the end of the 4th century. (DEA/G. DAGLI ORTI/Getty Images)

The Romans used spears – most commonly referred to as *hastae* (Ammianus, 25.3.6, 25.3.10, 27.10.12, 31.5.9 & 31.13.5), sometimes translated as lance; the term *pila* is not used. Ammianus mentions (31.13.8) a unit of *lanciarii* at the battle of Adrianople; in this we might argue that the *hasta* was a thrusting spear, whereas the *iaculum* (javelin) and perhaps *lancea* were missile weapons. For javelins, Ammianus specifically uses *iaculum* (31.10.19, 31.13.1, 31.15.13) but not *veru*, which also meant 'javelin'. We also find that the Romans used *plumbatae*, weighted darts; Vegetius (1.17) also uses the term *mattiobarbuli*. There is no evidence that the Goths adopted the *plumbata*, whereas for most other weapons we find that they used them as the Romans did. Ammianus uses the term *missilis* (24.6.10, 31.7.12, 31.10.8), which is usually translated as 'javelins' but can mean any thrown missile (so could mean *plumbatae*).

Another detail from the Arch of Galerius reveals decorated shields (both round and oval) and various armours. Here the emperor Galerius attacks Narses, the Sasanian king (r. 293–303). We can see ridge helmets with their distinctive crests behind the foreground figures. The armours here are a mix of tunics and 'muscled' cuirasses with *pteruges*, recalling an earlier period of Roman glory. (DE AGOSTINI PICTURE LIBRARY/Getty Images)

Lead *plumbata* heads from Enns in Austria. These are often called 'darts', but this term is misleading as *plumbatae* (also known as *mattiobarbuli* or *martiobarbuli*) were much larger. Vegetius, writing in the late 4th or early 5th century, mentions training with 'weighted javelins' (1.17). The wooden shafts have not been preserved, but they could be of various lengths. The only visual representation of a complete *plumbata* is a plate from the anonymous *De rebus bellicis*. The missiles would have been thrown upward so as to drop almost vertically on to enemy formations. (Wolfgang Sauber/ Wikimedia/CC BY-SA 3.0)

Slings were also used by both sides (Ammianus, 31.6.3, 31.7.14 & 31.15.13) and Vegetius (1.16) recommended Romans training in their use. Both sides used archery, although the Goths had proportionately higher numbers of archers and perhaps missile troops in general. We also find that the axe was used by both sides at the battle of Adrianople (Ammianus, 31.13.3); we find the Gothic axe in art and the Romans could carry a *securis* (the word Ammianus uses for both Roman and Gothic axes).

The archaeological record reveals that Gothic shield designs were hexagonal, but they also took and used Roman round and oval shields. In regard to shields we find Ammianus using the terms *clipeus* (24.6.10 & 25.3.8), *parma* (31.5.9) and *scutum* (25.3.3, 25.3.8, 25.3.10, 31.7.12 & 31.12.12) interchangeably, and seemingly without any differentiation between shape or size (at 25.3.8, *scutum* and *clipeus* are used to describe the same shield). The *clipeus* and *parma* were traditionally small and round.

Armour, too, is described by Ammianus using a variety of terms, including *lorica* (25.3.3 & 31.13.3); *arma* (24.2.8, 31.10.14, 31.13.1 & 31.13.7); *thorax*, for a breastplate (29.3.4); and *ferreus*, for 'iron' (29.3.4). The terms *hamata* (mail) and *squamata* (scale) are modern differentiations. Likewise, for helmets we find the catchall term *galea* used (26.6.16, 27.10.11 & 31.13.3).

In the battles of the Gothic Wars it is often difficult to discern tactics in the descriptions, even those provided by a military veteran such as Ammianus. Essentially, the Goths charged and the Romans resisted (or did not) until they broke. We do get some specifics, such as the *testudo* ('tortoise') formation used at the battle of the Willows (Ammianus, 31.7.12) and the use of the reserve there too. A Roman reserve also seems to have been deployed at the battle of Adrianople, in that case containing the *Batavi* – but it could not be found when needed (Ammianus, 31.13.9), or had already been rushed to a crisis point in the line. There are mentions of skirmishing, such as at the Willows (Ammianus, 31.7.11), conducted by troops who usually ranged ahead of the lines. On both sides there were probably javelinmen, archers and slingers. Archers also usually stood behind the heavy infantry (on both sides) to fire over them, but this is not entirely clear from Ammianus' narrative. Perhaps he expected his readers to know how Roman armies were drawn up – and he does warn us not to expect exacting details of the battles.

Ammianus' best description of armies deploying concerns the battle of Strasbourg or Argentoratum in 357 (16.12.1–70). It refers to several units with names which recurred during the Gothic Wars – the *Cornuti* and the *Batavi*, for instance. Heavy infantry drawn up in close ranks made up the bulk of most Roman armies, with cavalry on the wings. In many battle accounts this is not mentioned specifically; nor is it made clear whether the cavalry are light or heavy, or missile cavalry. It is possible that much more infantry was involved than cavalry at the battles of Marcianopolis and the Willows. In Ammianus' account of the battle of Adrianople we do find details of cavalry for the right wing (31.12.11); he reports (31.12.12) that the left wing never made it to the battlefield as it was still travelling. The condemnation in several sources of the lack of cavalry at Adrianople implies that the role of mounted troops was still important, if only to protect the flanks of the *legiones*.

Marcianopolis

AD 376

BACKGROUND TO BATTLE

Ammianus tells us (31.3.8) of the arrival of the Huns and their interaction with cultures as they moved westwards, noting that they were an unknown people, as does Eunapius (F41). Zosimus, in an all-too-brief summary, tells us (4.20.3) that a previously unknown 'barbarian' culture, the Huns, attacked the Scyths, who then begged to be accepted into the empire. Ammianus gives more detail, noting (31.2.13–15) that the nomadic Halani were a 'Scythian' people who bordered on the Greuthungi, Nervi, Vidini, Geloni, Agathyrsi, Melanchlaenae and Anthropophagi (the last were cannibals, we are told). Ammianus (31.2.15) actually identifies peoples who had contact with the Halani as far afield as the Seres – the 'silk-people', probably the northern Chinese – and the peoples of the Ganges. Many are just names, although Herodotus (4.104–09) also mentions several (though not the Halani). Against these peoples the Huns were unstoppable. The Halani were split between those who allied with the Huns and those who resisted. The latter were forced west, crossing the Dniester River (Ammianus, 31.3.3) under the leadership their child-king Viderichus, his affairs being managed by the commanders Alatheus and Saphrax. Having crossed the Dniester, the Halani came into conflict with the Theruingi and the Greuthungi.

The reverse of a *solidus* ('solid') coin showing Valens holding a *labarum* bearing the Chi Rho symbol. In other coin depictions of Valens and his contemporaries, the emperor is shown with typical equipment and wearing a 'muscled' cuirass with *pteruges*, cloak and boots. (York Museums Trust/Wikimedia/CC BY-SA 4.0)

The Theruingi were not unfamiliar to Valens. In 365–66 they had given support to the usurper Procopius and so Valens had campaigned against them north of the Danube (Ammianus, 27.5.1–2), although Ammianus refers to them simply as Goths at this point. Victor, Valens' *magister equitum* who would be present at the battle of Adrianople, had campaigned against the Goths previously (Ammianus, 27.5.1) and so was presumably familiar with their tactics. Valens also campaigned against the Greuthungi (Ammianus,

27.5.6), some of whom were ruled by Athanaric, who also seems to have been a leader among the Theruingi. This conflict, during which Fritigern wrested control from Athanaric, seems to have been the one mentioned by Sozomen (6.37) and Socrates (4.32), although these accounts show how the various peoples could be confused with one another.

When the Halani crossed the Dniester, the Theruingi attacked them, as they had promised the Romans they would do under the terms of the peace of 367, but the Huns attacked and defeated the Theruingi and the Greuthungi of Athanaric (Ammianus, 31.3.7–8). After this, Athanaric withdrew to the mountains; his people deserted him and looked to the fertile fields of Thrace as a refuge under the leadership of Alavivus (Ammianus, 31.4.1). Fritigern must have been one of the leaders of the Theruingi at this time, although in Ammianus' account we only meet him as they cross the Danube. From the northern bank of the Danube, these Goths sent word to Valens, begging to be allowed into the empire and promising that they would provide auxiliaries for the Roman Army. Ammianus notes (31.4.4) the activities of experienced flatterers at Valens' court, who spoke warmly of the emperor's good fortune in being promised so many young recruits with whom he could create an invincible army.

As we have seen, most of our sources for the Goths' activities in the later 370s tell us about their crossing of the Danube in 376 and then leap to the disaster of Adrianople in 378. At most the authors note that the Goths ravaged the areas of Moesia Secunda, Illyricum and Thrace, even parts of Macedonia, but only Ammianus seems to provide substantial detail of the events building up to the battle of Adrianople. We find slightly more information in Zosimus and Eunapius (and in one instance, Jordanes), although Eunapius' account is fragmentary; it would seem Zosimus was very brief in some parts of his narrative and that Eunapius' original provided much more detail.

Dating from between 293 and 304, this plinth from the Arch of Diocletian is now in the Boboli Gardens in Florence, Italy. It shows captured 'barbarian' arms consisting of scale armour and decorated shields. (Sailko/Wikimedia/ CC BY 2.5)

Sozomen (6.37) offers a slightly different version of events than that set out by Ammianus, stating that the Goths crossed the Danube first and only then despatched an embassy to Valens. Sozomen also records a civil war between the contingents led by Athanaric and Fritigern. In this version, Fritigern lost the initial conflict and appealed to Valens, promising to convert to the emperor's Arian form of Christianity; with Roman assistance Fritigern then defeated Athanaric and took command of the confederation of Goths. Certainly, Athanaric disappears from Ammianus' version of events. Socrates (4.32) offers a different version again, stating that the civil war among the Goths, in which Valens assisted Fritigern, occurred even before they were vanquished by the Huns. Zosimus states (4.34) that Fritigern led one element of the Goths (the other being led by Alatheus and Saphrax) to cross the Rhine River and threaten Gaul in 381 (see also Jordanes, *Getica* 140). After being allowed to leave the empire, they crossed back over the Danube into Pannonia and then warred with Athanaric again, perhaps for a final time; Athanaric went to the court of Theodosius I, but died soon after. Jordanes, however, states (142–44) that Athanaric succeeded Fritigern.

Ammianus tells us (31.4.1) that under Alavivus, the Theruingian Goths occupied the northern bank of the Danube and sent envoys to Valens, begging to be allowed to cross into the empire and promising that they would remain peaceful and provide auxiliary troops to the empire's armies if required. Rumours of an unknown culture (the Huns) causing havoc north of the Danube began to spread in the empire as well. The Gothic envoys confirmed this rumour (Ammianus, 31.4.4); the Romans received their requests with joy rather than fear, as it meant the Goths would provide many new recruits who might provide a bulwark against this new threat. This idea is confirmed in other accounts (Sozomen, 6.37; Socrates, 4.34). Ammianus mentions (31.4.4) the emperor's flatterers telling him he would have an invincible army and that the treasury would be filled, because these new recruits could be paid for by the provinces, which would not have to provide recruits themselves – a situation that had occurred in 359 (Ammianus, 19.11.7).

A Roman officer with a captive, possibly a Goth, from the Arch of Diocletian. Not much had changed in the Roman depiction of 'barbarians', hence the 'recycling' of the Dacians on Constantine I's own triumphal Arch of Constantine. The hairstyle matches those worn at the end of the 4th century. Tunics, cloaks and leggings did not change much either, and we continue to see officers wearing 'old fashioned' muscled cuirasses. (Sailko/Wikimedia/CC BY 2.5)

Ammianus states (31.4.5) that various officials were sent with vehicles to transport the horde across. Now that permission to cross had been granted, the entire population of the Goths took to whatever transport they could to traverse the Danube and settle in the Roman province of Thrace. The ferrying took several days and nights and Ammianus' account is full of foreboding: he notes that great efforts were made to appease the Goths, who were destined to defeat the might of Rome (31.4.5); letting them in was disastrous for Rome (31.4.6). Ammianus provides no numbers for the Goths crossing into the empire; the figure of 200,000 comes from Eunapius (F42). Ammianus, quoting Virgil (*Georgics* 2.106–08), simply compares the Goths to the numberless grains of sand and to the horde of Persians who had invaded Greece in 480 BC (31.4.6–7). According to Herodotus (7.185.3–186.2), the Persian invasion of 480 BC was undertaken by a contingent in excess of 5 million, with 2½ million of these being fighting men. No one believes Herodotus' numbers, but Ammianus clearly intended to convey the idea of a countless horde of Goths and uses their numbers to affirm that Herodotus may have been right. Ammianus informs us (31.4.8) that Fritigern and Alavivus of the Theruingi were allowed to enter Roman territory and that Valens ordered that they be provided with lands and given food. Ammianus does not mention the condition mentioned in the other sources (Zosimus, 4.20.6; Eunapius, F42) – that the Goths were required to hand over their weapons – instead describing the Goths as being armed.

MAP KEY

Marcianopolis, AD 376

1 The Theruingi Goths cross into the empire, over the Danube and into the Roman province of Moesia Secunda. They are most likely to have crossed at Durostorum, Appiaria or Sextaginta Prista.

2 After suffering extortion and deprivation at the hands of Lupicinus and Maximus, the Goths are marched to Marcianopolis, but are refused permission to buy provisions.

3 Lupicinus invites the Gothic leaders, Alavivus and Fritigern, to a banquet, his intention being to assassinate them. Outside the city, the Goths revolt and overpower their guards, taking their armour and weapons.

4 Fritigern manages to escape from the banquet and make his way back to the Goths; Alavivus is probably killed. Fritigern leads his warriors 15km away from the city, plundering as they go, probably north towards Durostorum; once there, he sends out the call for all Goths to join him.

5 Lupicinus gathers his forces at Marcianopolis and marches north to meet Fritigern's Goths.

6 The Goths gather into a single, angry mass, perhaps 30,000 strong. Most are unarmed and unarmoured (**A**).

7 Lupicinus (**B**), the *magister militum per Thracias*, advances with troops from the *comitatenses* based at Marcianopolis and the *limitanei* of Moesia Secunda, probably commanded by the *dux* Maximus (**C**). The Romans seem to have had no cavalry (except for officers and perhaps Lupicinus' bodyguard). The army consisted of *comitatus* infantry *legiones*, each of 1,000 men, and units of *vexillationes* and *auxilia*, each consisting of 500 men (**D**), as well as *legiones* from the *limitanei* consisting of 500 men each and units of *vexillationes* and *auxilia* of 250 men each (**E**). The total Roman force is, perhaps, 15,000 strong and advances in battle order.

8 Without allowing the Romans any time to prepare, the Goths charge the Roman line, despite being mostly unarmed and unarmoured.

9 The Goths throw themselves recklessly against the shields of the Romans, who are surprised at the ferocity of the Goths and are unable to recover.

10 The Goths press on, capturing the Roman standards. They cut down the Roman commander Maximus, the *tribuni*, and most of the soldiers, arming themselves with Roman weapons and taking up Roman shields and armour.

11 Lupicinus flees back to Marcianopolis.

12 After the battle, the Goths spread over Thrace. The Greuthungi cross the Danube, probably at Noviodunum in the province of Scythia.

Battlefield environment

Marcianopolis, the capital of the province of Moesia Secunda and the largest city in Thrace, lay 120km south of the Danube. The city was destroyed by Attila the Hun in 447 so its plan is remarkably intact. When Fritigern and Alavivus were taken inside the city, the remainder of the Goths were kept some distance from it. When the Goths rioted, however, they were able to assault the walls (although without equipment). We are told that Fritigern led the Goths 15km away from the city, presumably in the direction from which they had come – most probably northwards towards Appiaria or Durostorum (both on the Danube), or perhaps north-west towards Sextaginta Prista (on the Danube in Ruse, Bulgaria). This move will have taken the Goths perhaps as far as modern-day Vetrino or Suvorovo, where the ground is relatively flat. Modern-day Zlatina, approximately 15km to the west, encompasses more difficult terrain. The Goths may have blocked the Roman road north, in which case the road directly north to Durostorum (around modern-day Suvorovo) would seem the most likely site of the battle.

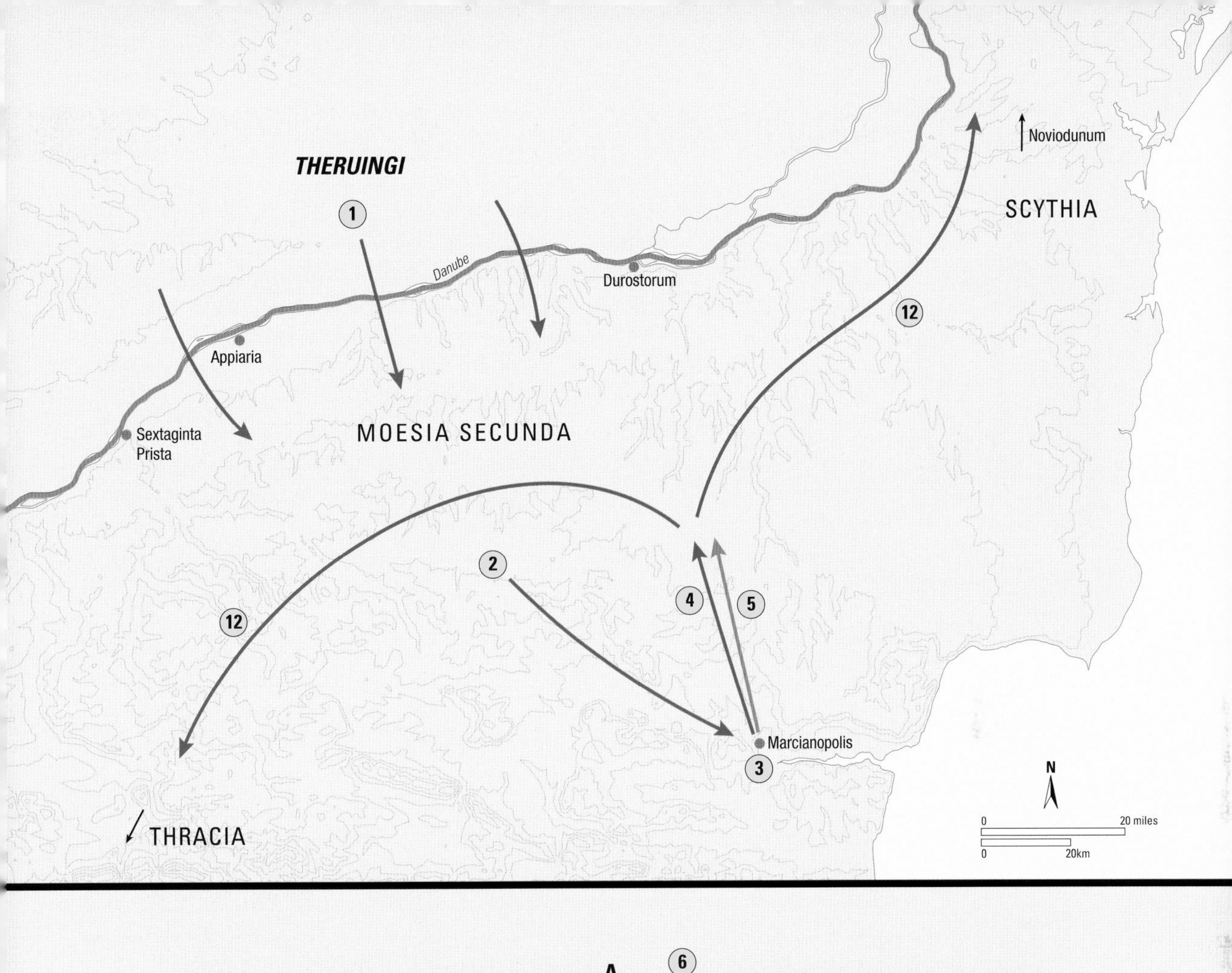
THERUINGI
1
Danube
Durostorum
Noviodunum
SCYTHIA
12
Appiaria
Sextaginta
Prista
MOESIA SECUNDA
2
4
5
12
Marcianopolis
3
THRACIA
N
0
20 miles
0
20km

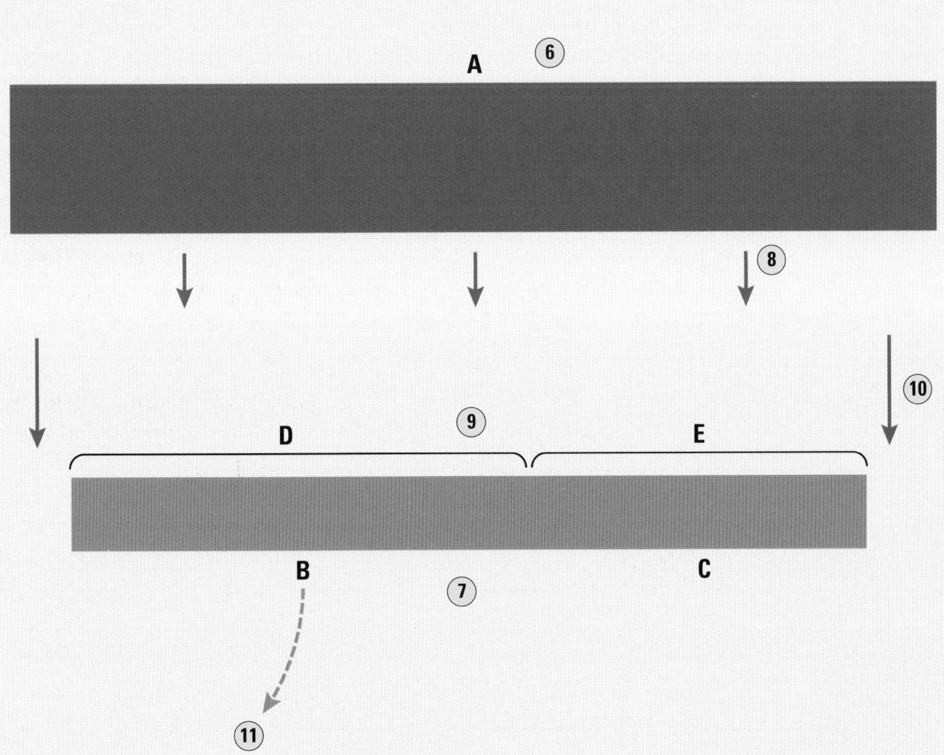
A
6
8
10
D
9
E
B
7
C
11

INTO COMBAT

Ammianus has damning words for the two men put in command of the armies of the provinces at this time. At a time when the empire needed the best possible men, command was given to men of impure character (31.4.9) who were notoriously wicked, ignorant and rash. These were Lupicinus, the *comes* of the diocese of Thrace, and the *dux* Maximus, presumably the *dux limitis* (commander of the *limitanei* border guards) of the province of Moesia Secunda (or perhaps the province of Scythia) into which the Goths crossed. More than the arrival of the Goths, Ammianus attributes the blame for the empire's woes to these two men's greed (31.4.10). Lupicinus and Maximus oversaw a rorting of the Goths for supplies – their demands including a slave as the price for a dog (for meat). Jordanes (134–35) also gives details of the extortion, claiming that a slave was the price for a loaf of bread; Ammianus only mentions bread later (31.6.5). Even the sons of the chieftains were traded in this way (Ammianus, 31.4.11; Jordanes, 135), perhaps as hostages.

Ammianus reveals (31.4.12) that more Goths were allowed to cross at this time, telling us that the child-king Vithericus and the Greuthungi, accompanied by Alatheus, Saphrax and Farnobius, asked to cross too. This contingent followed the Theruingi to the banks of the Danube and similarly asked Valens to be allowed to enter the empire, but at this juncture they were refused entry.

While Ammianus' version of events offers more detail than the other surviving accounts, the other authors provide a different explanation of such hostages; Eunapius (F42) has Valens order the taking of hostages, only then allowing others to cross once they had laid down their arms. Jordanes, Zosimus and Eunapius are also damning of the Roman commanders. Zosimus (4.20.6), following Eunapius, does not record the names of the Roman commanders as Ammianus does and omits several fragments of Eunapius' *Universal History*, which survive elsewhere, making it clear how much has been lost (see, for example, F42M). What is more, the picture presented is more simplistic than that conveyed by Ammianus' account. Zosimus records (4.20.6) that Valens agreed to allow the Goths to enter the empire if they gave up their weapons. In addition to Ammianus and Jordanes, Zosimus and Eunapius record the atrocities committed by the Roman commanders against the Goths, giving their revolt a cause. In the other (mainly ecclesiastical) sources, the accounts of which outnumber these four, the revolt was prompted by the Goths deliberately breaking their oaths. These ecclesiastical histories have accepted a Roman version of events in which the Romans did no wrong, whereas Ammianus and Jordanes, Zosimus and Eunapius present a more balanced view with blame attributed to both sides. Recording that the Roman commanders took slaves and workers for themselves and that some 'barbarians' entered the empire carrying arms, Zosimus claims (4.20.7) that the Goths moved into Thrace and Pannonia, reaching as far as Macedonia and Thessaly and plundering the countryside. Pannonia is not mentioned by Ammianus, nor is it mentioned in other fragments of Eunapius' work, but it is possible that Moesia Secunda is meant (as Zosimus omits Moesia Secunda, which they entered first).

The Theruingi, staying close to the banks of the Danube in the province of Thrace, were starving as a result of the neglect and corruption practised

THIS PAGE AND OPPOSITE The generic 'barbarians' depicted on the Arch of Constantine date from the reign of Trajan (r. 98–117) and represent Dacians of the early 2nd century. That they could be re-used on an arch in the 4th century shows that Roman perceptions of non-Romans had not changed much and, perhaps, that modes of 'barbarian' dress had not changed significantly either. (CristianChirita/Wikimedia/ CC BY-SA 3.0)

by the two Roman commanders. This caused anger and disaffection among the Goths (Ammianus, 31.5.1–2), but Lupicinus sent soldiers to escort them further into the empire, to Marcianopolis. When the Theruingi moved south, the Greuthungi took the opportunity to cross the Danube into the empire (Ammianus, 31.5.3), because there were so few Roman troops left close to the river to prevent them from doing so. In this context, Ammianus then offers (31.5.4) his first comment on Fritigern's cunning and foresight, stating that the advance of the Goths (towards Marcianopolis) was deliberately slow, while still obeying the order to march, in order to allow time for other Goths to cross. Jordanes (136) also commends this trait in Fritigern. At Marcianopolis, another Roman atrocity would lead to disaster for the empire.

The timing of the crossing of the Danube into Thrace is difficult to assess. Presumably, the Goths gathered in spring 376 and requested to be allowed to cross (or crossed and then asked, if we accept that tradition). The sending of a request to Valens and the subsequent Roman debate and response – as well as the Romans' poor conduct towards the Goths – must have taken some time; time enough for the Goths to use up all their provisions and become sufficiently desperate to fall prey to Roman extortions. The march to Marcianopolis probably began during the summer months, when there was still enough time to house and settle the Goths before it became too late in the year. With the delays mentioned by the ancient authors, the Goths' 120km march may have taken some time. Although there is no mention of climatic conditions in descriptions of the battle of Marcianopolis (as there would be in the chronicler's accounts of the battle of Adrianople), perhaps it took place in the late summer.

According to Ammianus (31.5.5), the Roman commanders, Lupicinus and Maximus, invited the leaders of the Goths, Alavivus and Fritigern, to a banquet inside the city. Lupicinus posted guards with the remaining Goths at some distance from the town. The Goths requested permission to go into the city to purchase food and provisions, but were refused. As they were now officially inhabitants of the empire, and had declared themselves to be loyal and obedient subjects, their frustration about the way they were being treated is understandable. The refusal to allow them to enter Marcianopolis led to arguments between the Goths and the Roman guards, which escalated into fights. When some of the Goths were then taken away by force, the violence became more widespread (Ammianus, 31.5.6).

Ammianus' description (31.5.5) is brief: the Goths' ferocity exploded and they slew some of the Roman guards, taking their weapons from them. Here Ammianus seems to suggest that the Goths were unarmed – something he neglected to mention at their crossing, but which is mentioned in several other sources. Some weapons must have made it across, whether smuggled or permitted, but the picture of unarmed Goths overpowering their unjust Roman guards makes the battle's beginning sound like a food riot that got out of hand. More was going on, however. Ammianus' version is that Lupicinus learned of the violence outside the city via a secret message (Ammianus, 31.5.6) and, even though drowsy and drunk, he ordered the honour-guard of Alavivus and Fritigern to be put to death as a precaution. This seems unlikely and it is more plausible that the banquet was staged as a means of assassinating Alavivus and Fritigern, in order to leave the Goths leaderless

and therefore make them easier to manage; this is the version of events recorded by Jordanes (135–36).

This detail from the Great Hunt mosaic shows examples of the decorated cloak and tunic, boots and undecorated shields. The owner of the villa (indicated by his staff) also wears a *pileus Pannonicus* (Pannonian hat), a style that became popular in the 3rd century. Note also the boots. The shields are probably undecorated because the men are not attached to any military unit, but their equipment would have been largely the same; decorated shields are also apparent on this mosaic. (DEA/G. DAGLI ORTI/Getty Images)

It seems that events outside the city escalated quickly, for we next hear of the Goths at the walls of the city, clamouring to get in (Ammianus, 31.5.7). They had learned of the death of the honour-guard and so renewed their violence, more and more joining their numbers as they looked to avenge their leaders, who they thought were being held captive. Once again, we get an insight into the quick thinking of Fritigern, a man of great resourcefulness (Ammianus, 31.5.7). Fearing he might be taken as a hostage, and arguing that there would be fighting and heavy loss of life, Fritigern persuaded Lupicinus to allow him to go to the Goths with his companions and calm them down (Ammianus, 31.5.7). Ammianus does not reveal the fate of Alavivus, but he is not mentioned again; he was either put to death or taken hostage. When Fritigern's request was granted, he made his way to the body of Goths, who welcomed him; then he withdrew them from the city.

An alternative version is recorded by Jordanes (136), who claims that Fritigern overheard the cries of his dying guards and thus perceived of the plot against him. He drew his sword and escaped, cutting his way through the perfidious Romans and rescuing those of his guards who were still alive. Despite the romanticism of Jordanes' account, it seems more likely than Fritigern being able to talk his way out of an assassination plot. Whatever the outcome, the Goths were incensed and, when word of what had happened at Marcianopolis spread, the entire nation of the Theruingi prepared for war, raising their battle-standards and sounding their war-trumpets (Ammianus, 31.5.8). Ammianus goes on to relate that the Goths now pillaged the countryside of Thrace and burned villages, taking by force the supplies they had been denied by the Roman commanders.

Lupicinus gathered his forces as rapidly as he could and advanced from Marcianopolis with more impetuosity than caution (Ammianus, 31.5.9). We do not know the length of time between the events at Marcianopolis and the subsequent battle, but it cannot have been long. Troops of the *comitatenses* were probably billeted around Marcianopolis, so gathering them should not have taken much time. The idea that Lupicinus' advance was rash also suggests that it was made soon after.

Some 15km from Marcianopolis, most likely to the north or north-west (the way the Goths had come), Lupicinus halted, ready to do battle. The Goths must have been drawn up awaiting the Roman advance, as we are told by Ammianus (31.5.9) that the Goths charged the Romans without any warning or regard for their own lives. Although the Romans were advancing in battle formation, this ferocious Gothic onslaught was unexpected. At just this

Here we see a slave and a lower-class worker depicted in the Great Hunt mosaic. The mosaic dates from the 4th century and is useful for detail of clothing and their colours – a relatively rare trait in surviving ancient art. The tunic and boots offer useful indications about the styles worn by members of the lower classes, unlike most other surviving art, which depicts rulers or their (elite) guards. (DEA/ARCHIVIO J. LANGE/Getty Images)

moment, however, Ammianus' Latin becomes difficult to interpret (31.5.9), but it would seem that the Goths rushed their enemy, threw themselves bodily against the Romans' shields and then cut them down with swords, spears or whatever weapons came to hand. The Goths, especially if some were unarmed and unarmoured, must have outnumbered the Romans, perhaps by at least 2 to 1; even so, their charge was unexpected. The Goths were also suffering the effects of famine and depravation, so would not have been expected to fight effectively. It would seem that it was the ferocity of the attack which surprised the Romans, perhaps compounded by the fact that some of the attackers were unarmed and unarmoured. Another reading is that the Goths charged into the Roman ranks recklessly with their shields. Whichever interpretation is correct, the onslaught of the Goths surprised the Romans and they were cut down.

The Gothic attack did not abate and they continued on until they had captured the Roman standards and cut down the Roman *tribuni* and the majority of the soldiers (Ammianus, 31.5.9). Lupicinus fled the field – probably on horseback – and retreated as fast as he could to Marcianopolis. The Goths took the arms and armour of the Romans they had killed – an act which implies that many of the Goths had gone into battle without adequate arms or armour – and continued their rampage.

Unfortunately, Ammianus – who, with Jordanes, is the only historian to give any detail about the battle at Marcianopolis – gives us no sense of the numbers involved on either side. Immediately following his account of the battle, Ammianus tells us (31.5.10) not to expect exact numbers of the slain from him, or a strictly accurate account of what took place, because it was impossible to know. There are some clues to the numbers of men involved, however. Ammianus tells us (31.5.10) how the Goths were numberless; he mentions that Lupicinus summoned his troops quickly, but we do not know how many Roman troops there were. As the *comes* of the diocese of Thrace, Lupicinus commanded the *comitatenses* centred on Thrace, and Marcianopolis was the force's base. If we assume there to have been 1,000 men per *legio* and 500 men per *vexillatio* or unit of *auxilia*, the Roman force amounted to some 27,000 men in total.

Lupicinus could also have summoned men from the *limitanei* of both Moesia Secunda and Scythia – Maximus was *dux* of one of those provinces, most probably Moesia Secunda – although they were some distance away. This would have provided another 15,000 men (based on 500 men per *legio* and 250 for each of the other units). It is unlikely that Lupicinus had 40,000 men at Marcianopolis, however, as deploying such a force would have denuded the entire diocese of troops, but he probably had some men from the *limitanei* of Moesia Secunda. Many others must have remained in their garrisons. At the same time, however, it seems clear that there were few troops left in Moesia Secunda or Scythia to prevent the crossing of the Greuthungi, and so many of the men of that army were presumably guarding the Theruingi during their march to Marcianopolis. Men of the *comitatenses* under Lupicinus were probably used for that guard duty too; and the Goths did capture more than one standard.

Given the devastations which were to flow on throughout Thrace as a result of the Roman defeat at Marcianopolis, we might err on a higher figure for troop numbers rather than a lower figure. Some modern scholars place the Roman force at 5,000 men and the Goths at 10,000, but these are (low) guesses. If we assume that most of the *limitanei* (7,000–8,000 men) were fielded and that some of the *comitatenses* were summoned – perhaps the same number again, one-third of Lupicinus' forces – we arrive at a figure of about 15,000 men on the Roman side.

At the same time, the armies of Thrace would continue to supply men in all of the battles until Adrianople, so that army cannot have been wiped out. Certainly, Ammianus follows his account of the battle of Marcianopolis with a long digression (31.5.12–17) comparing this battle with all of the great calamities of 'barbarian' invasions that had befallen Rome beforehand. Even taking hyperbole and exaggeration into account, we might expect that the defeat was calamitous (even though much worse was to follow). Nevertheless, by comparing the disaster to the invasion of the Cimbri and Teutones in the late 2nd century BC and subsequent upheavals, Ammianus ensures that we should not underestimate the invasion of 376. He also warns (31.5.14) that, whereas in times past Rome restored its fortunes through old virtues, now Rome's armies were infected with effeminacy and licentiousness, which would result in even greater disasters to come. This warning also gives us pause to consider the works of Vegetius and others, which looked to restore just those virtues of old to the Roman state.

Lupicinus and Maximus disappear from Ammianus' narrative at this point, no doubt replaced in command. Jordanes, however, tells us (137) that Fritigern killed them both, which contradicts Ammianus' version of Lupicinus' fate. Jordanes gives more detail on the battle of Marcianopolis than on the battle of Adrianople, which receives only the briefest treatment.

The Willows

AD 377

BACKGROUND TO BATTLE

As we have seen, there were already Goths serving in Roman armies prior to 376. After the battle of Marcianopolis, however, several of these contingents rebelled. Ammianus tells us (31.6.1–3) of the Gothic commanders Sueridus and Colias, based in winter quarters at Adrianople, who did not, at first, join with their Gothic brethren. When they were ordered by Valens to cross the Hellespont and they asked for provisions for the journey, the chief magistrate armed the population against them and expelled them from the city. Only at this point did the Goths in Adrianople rebel and they attacked those citizens armed against them, probably arming themselves and plundering the *fabricia* (arms factory) there. The Goths also equipped themselves from the slain and joined Fritigern in placing the city under siege.

Fritigern soon realized that the Goths were unsuited to sieges and advised them to blockade the city and ravage the countryside. Ammianus gives Fritigern a pithy comment to sum up this policy, stating that 'he did not make war with stone walls' (31.6.4). This statement places Fritigern within a long tradition of laconic statements uttered by great generals stretching all the way back to the 5th century BC. Ammianus surmises (31.6.5) that the Goths then spread all over Thrace and plundered, largely unchecked, informed by prisoners as to the location of rich villages and supplies of food. In this, we find a further point shared by most of the sources that cover this period so briefly: Gothic slaves (including those traded when they first arrived) and others (including those who worked in the mines of Thrace and Macedonia) flocked to Fritigern, swelling the Goth numbers yet further (Ammianus, 31.6.5–6).

When Valens was informed of this, he sent Victor, his *magister equitum*, to Persia to make diplomatic arrangements while he prepared to leave

This marble bust of either Gratian or his half-brother Valentinian II dates from *c.*375. Gratian was Western Roman Emperor from 367 until 383. The eldest son of Valentinian I (and therefore Valens' nephew), Gratian had almost grown up in the Roman Army, accompanying his father's campaigns on the Rhine and Danube before he was 16. He was that age when his father died in 375 and he became emperor – although he had been given the title of *augustus* in 367, when he was only eight. (Universal History Archive/ Getty Images)

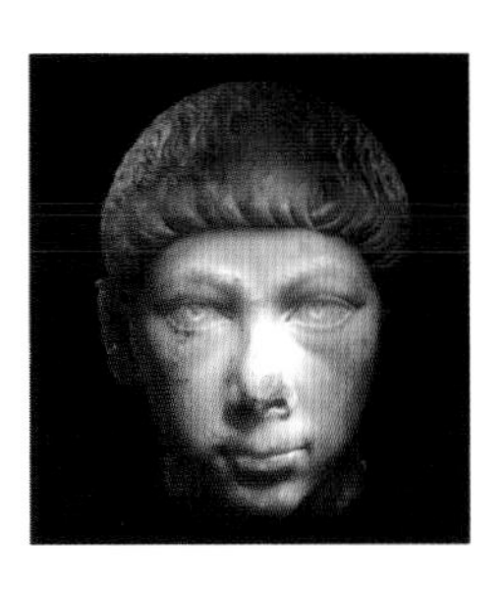

These soldiers depicted on the Arch of Constantine are storming a city and, like the Goths, seem to have no specialist siege equipment. Fritigern realized the futility of the Goths engaging in sieges and tended to avoid them, although he did unsuccessfully besiege Constantinople after his victory at Adrianople. (DEA/ARCHIVIO J. LANGE/ Getty Images)

Antioch himself and return to Constantinople (Ammianus, 31.7.1). Ahead of this, he sent the commanders Profuturus and Traianus, presumably to replace Lupicinus and Maximus, although Traianus was *magister peditum* and so outranked the *comes* Lupicinus. Ammianus is damning of both men, calling them ambitious, but not particularly skilled in war (31.7.1). This verdict belies Traianus' seemingly stellar career to that point; he had been *dux Aegypti* (commander of forces in Egypt) in the 360s and *comes rei militaris* (a military commander superior to a *dux*, but below a *magister peditum* or *magister equitum*) against the Persians in the early 370s. Profuturus would perhaps be among the fallen at the battle of the Willows, and Traianus would die at the battle of Adrianople. Ammianus states (31.7.2) that these commanders arrived with *legiones* brought from Armenia and, rather than use ambushes and surprises and defeat the enemy in detail which better

This detail from the Arch of Constantine shows figures wearing Pannonian hats and cloaks; we also see a wagon. Evidence suggests that Roman soldiers may sometimes have gone into combat wearing long tunics only rather than armour. (Prisma/Universal Images Group/Getty Images)

This battle scene from the Arch of Constantine shows Roman cavalry wearing long tunics defeating enemies wearing scale armour and driving them into a river. The enemy cavalrymen have smaller, convex round shields. (DEA/ARCHIVIO J. LANGE/ Getty Images)

suited the terrain, they chose to oppose the Goths in a pitched battle. The army based in Armenia was the same size as that in Scythia and Moesia Secunda. The transfer of *legiones* from this army to Thrace in 377 might suggest that most of the *limitanei* of Moesia Secunda had been wiped out at the battle of Marcianopolis.

Again, Ammianus states (31.7.3) that the Goths were innumerable, but also fuelled by rage and despair – something which the *legiones* from Armenia had not encountered before. The Goths also occupied all the high ground and plains. They retreated to Mount Haemus, where the Romans hoped to starve them yet further. The Romans also awaited the arrival of the *dux* Frigiderius, despatched from Pannonia by Gratian with several units of *auxilia*. Valens had requested this assistance, which suggests that the Romans recognized the scale of the threat posed by the Goths and that there was a concerted effort from both West and East to combat it.

Gratian also sent Richomeres, his *comes domesticorum*, from Gaul. Richomeres brought several cohorts of *protectores* and *protectores domestici*; these were below strength, however, perhaps as a result of desertions or because some men had been kept back in Gaul lest their absence prove too tempting for the Germanic peoples on the other side of the Rhine (Ammianus, 31.7.4). A cohort was usually 500 men at full strength, so perhaps half that strength may have been despatched to the East – or possibly 300 men per cohort, using Ammianus (20.4.2) as a guide. As Frigiderius was suffering an attack of gout (or pretending to), command of all the Roman forces in Thrace was offered to Richomeres (Ammianus, 31.7.5). Profuturus and Traianus placed themselves under his leadership. They were encamped at the town of Ad Salices ('by the willows').

The Willows, AD 377

MAP KEY

1 The Goths summon their predatory bands back to the wagon laager, perhaps by fire (or smoke) signal, perhaps by war-trumpet. They arrive before nightfall, but too late in the day for action.

2 The Romans do not sleep, expecting some Gothic trick. The 'countless' (Ammianus, 31.7.2) Goths outnumber the Romans.

3 At first light the following day, both sides sound their war-trumpets. The Goths (**A**) proceed to higher ground to give more impetus to their charge. The Gothic archers and slingers (**B**) are drawn up behind and the Gothic cavalry (**C**) wait to cut down those Romans who flee.

4 The Romans (**D**), consisting of understrength units of *auxilia* and cohorts of troops from Richomeres and Frigiderius as well as the *legiones*, *vexillationes* and *auxilia* of Profuturus and Traianus, stay in a single body and advance slowly towards the enemy before halting. A strong Roman reserve (**E**) waits behind the main body.

5 The Romans raise their *barritus* war-cry and the Goths shout back in response. The Goths attempt to skirmish with the Romans and missiles – javelins, *plumbatae* and arrows – are exchanged.

6 Both sides rush to close combat. The Romans form a *testudo* formation with their entire army. The Goths charge the *testudo* and launch large volumes of missiles against it.

7 Using huge clubs, the Goths break the *testudo* and defeat the left wing of the Roman formation.

8 The Roman reserve shores up the Roman line and prevents its collapse.

9 The Romans hold out and fighting is fierce. Eventually, some break and run, only to be cut down by the Gothic cavalry. As night falls, the Romans withdraw to their camp, the Goths to their wagon laager.

Battlefield environment

The location of Ad Salices is unknown. Some clues are provided in the *Antonine Itinerary*, however, in that a town called Ad Salices ('by the willows') was located between Tomis and Salmuris. Salmuris has defied identification, although some locate it north of Tomis. After the battle, however, the Romans withdrew to Marcianopolis and so it is possible that Ad Salices was located closer to Marcianopolis, perhaps on the road to Durostorum, north of Marcianopolis on the Danube.

The historian Edward Gibbon placed Ad Salices almost 100km north of Tomis, which cannot be correct. We might locate Ad Salices in a triangle between Tomis, Durostorum and Marcianopolis, encompassing eastern parts of modern-day Romania and Bulgaria. The name implies both the presence of willow trees and a plentiful water supply as well as a hill on which the Goths built their wagon laager and another to which the Gothic infantry moved before the battle.

As for establishing the time of year of the battle, the one clue we get from Ammianus is that these events occurred towards autumn (31.8.2).

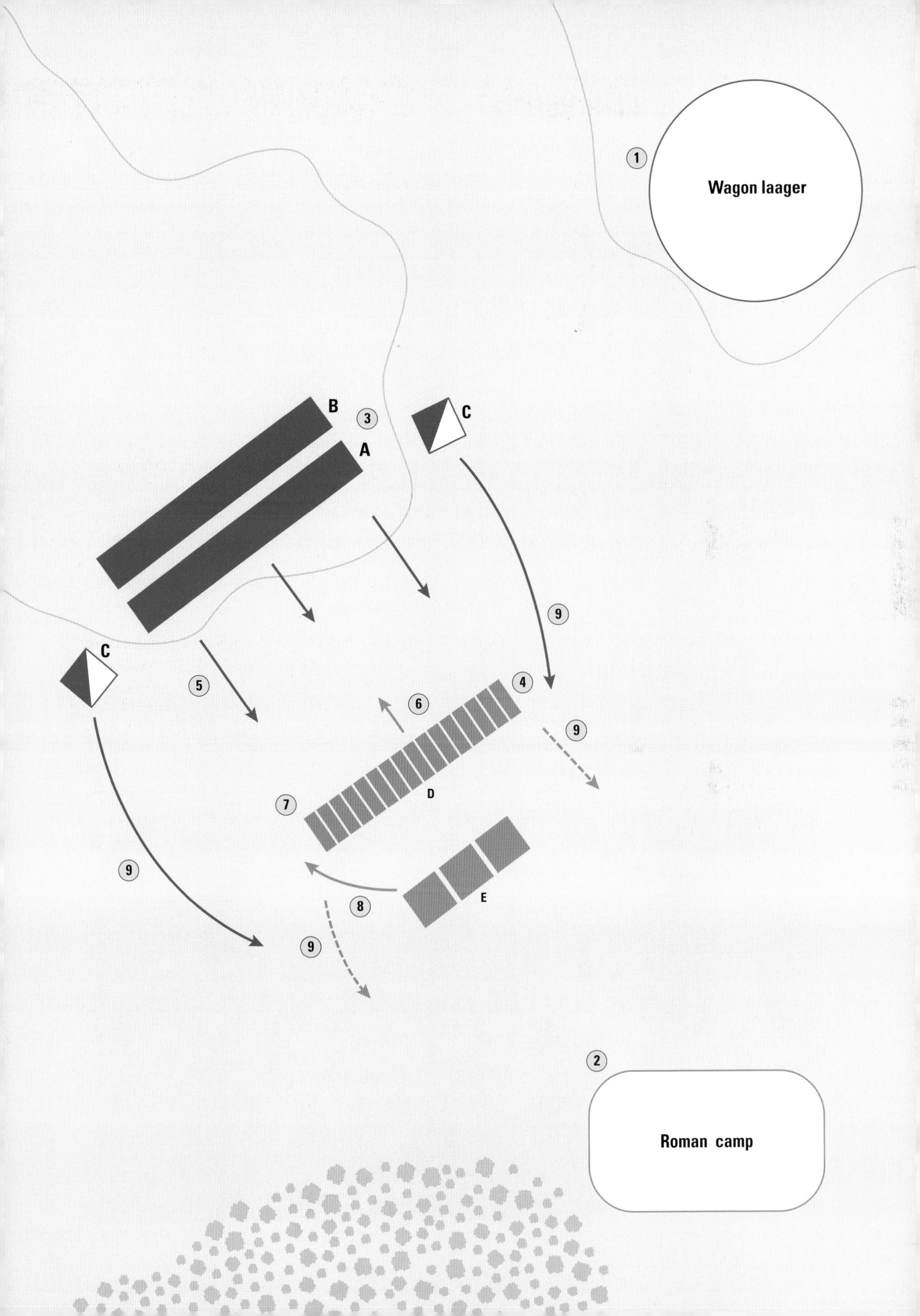

1
Wagon laager
B
3
C
A
9
C
5
4
6
9
D
7
9
8
E
9
2
Roman camp

INTO COMBAT

Not far from Ad Salices, the Goths had built their wagon laager on a hill, drawn up in a circle (Ammianus, 31.7.5) within which they enjoyed their spoils from plundering the countryside. The Romans kept a keen eye on the Goths from their camp close by, watching for an opportunity to perform some intrepid deed (Ammianus, 31.7.6) and to shadow any movement of the Gothic camp. If the Goths moved camp – and such movements were a common habit – the Romans could fall upon their rear and kill as many as they could – and recover as much booty as possible. The Goths became aware of this eventuality (Ammianus, 31.7.7), possibly being informed of the prospect by deserters, and so stayed in the one location.

Ammianus tells us (31.7.7) that the Goths were afraid of the Roman force opposing them, but this seems unlikely given the Goths' success the year before, and they would have seen nothing to change their mind concerning the quality of the Roman troops opposing them. The Goths summoned their predatory bands, which were roaming the countryside, back to the wagon laager by signal. What this signal was we are not told – possibly one organized in advance or one characteristic of their culture (Ammianus, 31.7.7). It has been speculated that the signal could have been the 'sorrowful trumpets' (*triste sonatibus classicis*) mentioned by Ammianus (31.5.8), in which case they may well also have been used to summon Gothic forces before the battle of Marcianopolis. The instruction to return to the wagon laager may also have been conveyed via fire or smoke signals. If this was the case, then it makes what happened at the battle of Adrianople more interesting (Ammianus, 31.12.13). Whatever the nature of the signal was, the rampaging bands reacted as soon as they were called for and returned before nightfall, so they could not have been too far away. The return of these bands encouraged the Goths to attempt something daring (Ammianus, 31.7.8), but it was deemed to be too late in the day to initiate action.

The Ludovisi Sarcophagus, dating from the mid-3rd century, shows a wealth of detail of equipment and armour, the use of which continued into the 4th century. Note the various styles of Roman helmet (also depicted on the Arch of Constantine) and different shields and armours – especially the mail tunic on the right. The Roman swords depicted are shorter *gladii* rather than the long *spathae* wielded by their opponents. (Jastrow/Wikimedia/Public Domain)

A detail from the Great Hunt mosaic showing a 4th-century Roman cart. The Gothic wagons would likely have been very similar. According to Ammianus (31.2.18, 31.7.5, 31.12.11 & 31.15.5), the Goths lived in their wagons and circled them into wagon laagers. (DE AGOSTINI PICTURE LIBRARY/Getty Images)

The Romans did not sleep that night (Ammianus, 31.7.9), but were wary of some escapade by the Goths during the night; Ammianus comments (31.7.9) on the Roman fears of the Goths and their deranged (*male sanus*) leaders. In the same chapter, Ammianus notes that although the Romans knew they were outnumbered by the Goths, the emperor's men trusted in the justness of their cause. This acceptance of inferior Roman numbers when facing 'barbarian' (or indeed Persian) forces is something which Vegetius also mentions. He too accepted that the Romans would be outnumbered, but opens his *Epitoma rei militaris* with the admonishment (1.1) that it is not weight of numbers or untaught bravery which win victory but skill, training and discipline.

As soon as it was light the next day (Ammianus, 31.7.10), both sides raised war-trumpet calls to take up arms. The Goths swore an oath to their standards and then proceeded to higher ground as it would give additional impetus to their charge as they sought to overwhelm their enemy. In response, the Romans took up their positions, each man at his own station; Ammianus uses the term *maniple* (31.7.10), a very old-fashioned term. Once in place the Roman force stood firm and its troops did not leave ranks or move to charge the enemy.

Another wagon from the Great Hunt mosaic. There is some variety in the design of these wagons, even in an 'idealized' artwork. This is to be expected in a pre-industrial society and so, while such items may have had a broadly similar appearance, and presumably Gothic wagons looked much the same, there will have been variations. (Codex/Wikimedia/ CC BY-SA 4.0)

Roman infantry and cavalry on the march. Long tunics and equipment are clearly depicted, including several designs of helmet. None of these designs seem to reflect the *spangenhelm* style that was becoming more widespread, but it may not have been an artistic convention. This in itself is slightly odd, however, as the contemporary round shield and long tunics of the soldiers are depicted. (Prisma/ Universal Images Group/Getty Images)

Ammianus tells us (31.7.11) that both sides advanced cautiously towards one another and then halted, staring each other down silently with fierce, warlike looks (*torvitate mutua bellatores luminibus*). In unison, the Romans raised their war-cry, the *barritus*. According to Ammianus (31.7.11), the *barritus* started low and soft and then rose in pitch and volume. This is one of the most revealing references to the Late Roman war-cry; there are others (Ammianus, 16.12.43, 21.13.15 & 26.7.17; Vegetius, 3.18.9). There is evidence of war-cries in Roman armies stretching back to the Republic, and Rome's opponents commonly employed them too. The *barritus* was probably of Germanic origin and the term is also used to describe an elephant's trumpet call, first being used by units of *auxilia palatina* and catching on from there. Vegetius admonishes (3.18.9) that such a cry should only be made after the sides have engaged, although Ammianus points out (31.7.11) that at the Willows, the cry motivated and encouraged the Romans before they made contact with the enemy. In response, the Goths shouted back the accomplishments of their ancestors and yelled discordantly, in contrast with the unison of the Romans. Several sections of the Gothic force then attempted to engage the Romans in skirmishes (this may cast light on the escalation that would occur at the battle of Adrianople). Missiles were then exchanged; Ammianus specifically mentions javelins (31.7.12), and other missiles would have included *plumbatae* and arrows. Then the two sides rushed to close combat with shouts.

Ammianus tells us (31.7.12) that the Romans packed their shields together in a *testudo* ('tortoise') formation, and in this formation they came toe to toe with the Goths. This is fascinating as the actual use of the *testudo* in Roman battles is rarely recorded in the sources. In art (on both the columns of Trajan and Marcus Aurelius) the *testudo* is shown during Roman assaults on enemy fortifications, but in Ammianus' account – as with Plutarch's and Cassius Dio's accounts of Mark Antony's campaign against Parthia in 36 BC, more than 400 years earlier – we read of the *testudo* being used in open battle. What is more, while the *testudo* is familiar for its use of the curved rectangular *scutum* (as depicted on the aforementioned columns), both Antony's and the *testudo* at the Willows would have been made with flat oval and circular shields.

A cast of the *testudo* formation depicted on Trajan's Column, now in the Muzeul National de Istorie a României. Ammianus explicitly tells us (31.7.12) that the Romans adopted a *testudo* formation at the battle of the Willows and even though the round and oval shields of the 4th century seem less well suited to such a formation than the curved rectangular *scutum* of the 1st and 2nd centuries, Roman *legiones* must still have been capable of adopting such a formation. Mark Antony's forces, bearing oval shields, deployed a *testudo* in Parthia in 36 BC (Plutarch, *Mark Antony* 45.2–3; Cassius Dio, 49.29.2–31.1). (CristianChirita/Wikimedia/ CC BY-SA 3.0)

Ammianus simply uses the term *testudo* as if his readers would be familiar with it, unlike his glossing of other terms such as *clibanarii* and even *barritus*. Similarly, he does not gloss the term *cuneus* ('wedge') when he uses it. We can use descriptions of Antony's *testudo*, however, to better understand the

A Roman *testudo* formation depicted on the Column of Marcus Aurelius in Rome, again made with curved rectangular *scuta*. This is one of the only two surviving depictions of the *testudo* formation in action (the other being on Trajan's Column), and in both cases the formation is being used to assault walls. At the battle of the Willows, however, the *testudo* formation was used to enable the Romans to absorb the missiles of the more numerous Goths, showing that it could also be a formation suited to the open battlefield. (DEA/ARCHIVIO J. LANGE/Getty Images)

Fritigern

The Gothic leader Fritigern (or Fridigern, perhaps based on the Gothic Frithugairns) is one of the most under-appreciated commanders of the ancient world. At the head of a complex confederation of Gothic groups and having steered his people out of trouble north of the Danube, he would be responsible for Gothic successes since 376, imposing a series of devastating defeats on the forces of the Western Roman Empire that culminated at the battle of Adrianople.

Fritigern emerges into history just prior to, or at, the time that the Huns were pushing the Goths south towards the Danube. Ammianus provides no information about Fritigern's background when he is introduced by that author; the church historians Sozomen and Socrates introduce him earlier, in order to deal with his conversion to Arian Christianity. Fritigern led a smaller contingent of Theruingi Goths in opposition to Athanaric, but was defeated in some kind of civil conflict. He appealed to Rome, and, with Valens' help, won primacy in a second bout of conflict.

With Alavivus, Fritigern led the Theruingi's crossing of the Danube in 376. Fritigern also seems to have been the mind behind the offer to become soldiers for the empire in return for land to settle. Alavivus disappears from the narrative after Marcianopolis in 376, presumably murdered by the Roman commander Lupicinus. Thereafter it was Fritigern who was the mastermind of Gothic tactics and strategy, especially at the Willows and at Adrianople. There were other Gothic leaders (such as Alatheus, Saphrax and Farnobius) but they seem to have cooperated with Fritigern's wishes and perhaps deferred to his leadership.

The sources are full of (grudging) Roman admiration for Fritigern's leadership and abilities, and Ammianus and Jordanes tell us that he was full of trickery. It is this which suggests that the course of events at the battle of Adrianople was all part of a deliberate plan by Fritigern to lure Valens and the Roman forces he led into a carefully laid trap.

Fritigern disappears from the narrative soon after the battle of Adrianople (he is last mentioned by Ammianus at 31.16.3), and we do not know his fate, although Zosimus (4.36) and Jordanes (140) have him still as leader in early 381, the last time he is mentioned.

formation in use at the battle of the Willows – especially given that the equipment was so similar. The size and shape of Antony's shields would have been remarkably similar to those used by Richomeres' troops at the Willows, and the *testudo* in use at the latter battle may have been formed in the same way. Plutarch (*Antony* 45.2) does not use the term *testudo* itself, but describes it as being formed by the first rank dropping to one knee and holding their shields in front of them, the second rank holding their shields over the rank of the first and the third doing likewise. This created the appearance of a roof of shields, which offered remarkable protection against arrows.

Cassius Dio's description of Mark Antony's campaigns (49.29.2–31.1) adds more detail; he uses the term *testudo* and cites the formation as a defence against arrows. Shields were joined and the front rank knelt, but Cassius Dio describes the front rank as being made of curved shields, which were common in his own era (the late 2nd and early 3rd centuries) but which did not exist in Antony's day. Cassius Dio then describes the roof of the formation as being made of flat shields above everyone's heads. He describes its strength (49.30.3–4), stating that men could walk on the roof of shields and horses and vehicles could even be driven on it, and says it was used in two ways – to assault walls or when surrounded by archers, as Antony was (and Richomeres was in 377). This suggests – as Vegetius would later state (1.20) – that the Goths had many archers.

Another point to note is that both Antony and Richomeres seem to have called upon their entire body of infantry to form the *testudo* against the onslaught of the enemy, not just a small part of their force (as depicted on the column reliefs). Roman infantry may have drawn up in ranks 8–10 men

Richomeres

Flavius Richomeres was a Frankish commander who forged a successful career in the armies of both the Western and Eastern Roman empires. Of all the commanders to face the Goths in the 370s, he, arguably, had the most success.

When Richomeres first appears in the historical record (Ammianus, 31.7.4) it as the *comes domesticorum* of Gratian in Gaul, despatched to Thrace to assist Valens with some understrength cohorts of *protectores* and *protectores domestici*. He must have had a stellar career already, given his senior position at the Western court; upon his arrival in Thrace, by common consent he was given command of all the Roman forces gathered before the battle of the Willows. The cooperation apparent between West and East in his taking over command is quite remarkable. It is possible, however, that Frigiderius (also from the West) took issue with having to serve under Richomeres and avoided taking the field, using an attack of gout as an excuse. What is more, when the Romans' battlefield record against the Goths before the battle of Adrianople is considered, only Richomeres and Sebastianus seem to have had any success and Sebastianus' were in (deliberately) small-scale encounters. Sebastianus' career is also problematic in the sources, which offer contradictory details.

Richomeres returned to the West at the end of 377 in order to bring yet more troops from Gaul the following year. Again, he would be sent east in advance of Gratian to take part in the Adrianople campaign. Once again, he played a prominent role, volunteering to go as a hostage to the Gothic wagon laager, and was one of only a few of Rome's senior commanders who escaped the battle of Adrianople alive.

Richomeres was probably involved in the final peace negotiations with the Goths in 382. He was made *magister militum per orientem* (master of soldiers of the East) by Theodosius I in 383 and consul in 384. He was a pagan and was promoted on the basis of his abilities, becoming *comes et magister utriusque militae* (supreme commander of the army) in the East in 388, and remaining in this role until his death in 393. He fought against the usurper Magnus Maximus in 388 and died just before he could go into battle against another usurper, Eugenius (Zosimus, 4.55.2–3; Themistius, *Oration 16*: 201; Libanius, *Oration 1*: 219; Philostorgius, 10.8).

deep, so a *legio* of 1,000 men would have a frontage of 100–125 men. The *testudo* therefore would have been six to eight ranks deep, with the first rank kneeling, the second rank holding their shields over the first and the third and subsequent ranks forming the roof; the men on the extreme right must have swapped their shields to their right arms.

Ammianus describes (31.7.12) how the Goths, using huge *clavae* (clubs) hardened in fire, broke into the *testudo* and killed the men there with sword thrusts. This technique eventually broke the left wing of the Roman formation. The men there fell back towards a strong reserve (Ammianus, 31.7.12), the troops of which came up and supported the left wing just as it was about to give way. The implication is that the Goths, while not entirely surrounding the Romans, could certainly threaten the leftmost elements of the Roman formation, which was only saved by the quick action of bringing up the reserve.

Ammianus tells us (31.7.13) that after this, the battle raged with vast slaughter. Again, individual Goths threw themselves against the shields of the Romans, hoping to break their formation. Arrows and javelins filled the air (Ammianus, 31.7.13) and sword-blows were rapid. The cavalry (Ammianus, 31.7.12 – the first time they are mentioned) cut down any who fled; the infantry stabbed those who tried to flee on foot from behind or hamstrung them. This description does not make it clear on which side the fleeing and pursuing occurred, but it seems more likely that Roman troops attempted to get away from the fighting and so it is probably the Gothic cavalry which is meant.

PREVIOUS PAGES

The Battle of the Willows

The Romans, commanded by the Frank Richomeres, *comes domesticorum* in the West, have advanced their combined forces of Western and Eastern Roman troops towards the town of Ad Salices ('by the willows'), where the Goths have drawn up their circular wagon laager. Despite the Goths' superior numbers, the Romans have joined battle early on an August morning. The Romans have formed into a defensive *testudo* formation, locking their shields together to withstand the many missiles of the Goths. Having occupied a small hill to give impetus to their charge, the Goths assail the *testudo* with missiles of all kinds, including huge clubs hurled to break the shield-wall formation, shouting slogans as they do so. On their right they have managed to reach the *testudo* and are striving to pull the formation apart with their bare hands, killing the Romans there with *spathae* and axes. A reserve of Roman infantry moves to this point of crisis in the *testudo*. The Roman *labarum* (standard) bearing the Chi Rho symbol of each unit can be seen behind the *testudo* formation.

Ammianus describes the whole field as being filled with corpses and those half-alive (31.7.14), wounded by sling bullets (their first mention) and arrows, who lay among the dead. Others had their heads caved in or nearly severed from sword-blows. It is a most visceral description. The fighting continued until evening (Ammianus, 31.7.15) and only darkness put an end to the battle. The fierce action described by Ammianus seems too intense to have taken place continuously from soon after sunrise until darkness fell during the late summer. Perhaps the *testudo* formation stood, impervious to archery-fire, for some hours. In the darkness, the Goths withdrew with no order back to their wagon laager and the Romans withdrew, full of sorrow (Ammianus, 31.7.15), back to the tents of their camp.

Once again, Ammianus gives us no sense of the numbers involved other than the idea that the Goths outnumbered the Romans. On the Roman side there were units of *auxilia* brought from Pannonia by Frigiderius, *legiones* brought from Armenia by Profuturus and Traianus, and the understrength cohorts of Richomeres. Perhaps the numbers were again similar to those taking the field at Marcianopolis; Ammianus notes (31.7.2) that small-unit actions were better suited to this terrain, but that was not the course the Romans pursued. We can perhaps also surmise that, whatever the numbers of Roman troops present at Marcianopolis and the Willows, the numbers

RIGHT
The gilt copper and iron helmet from the Gammertingen find is now in the Landesmuseum Württemberg in Stuttgart, Germany. The decoration suggests the appearance of the most decorative examples of such helmets. (Daderot/Wikimedia/Public Domain)

FAR RIGHT
A mid-4th-century Roman ridge helm with the cheek pieces missing. Coins dating from the late 3rd century onwards show ridge helmets with high crests; the crests shown on the *missorium* of Valentinian I correspond to such types. (Sailko/Wikimedia/CC BY-SA 3.0)

FAR LEFT
This highly decorated ridge helmet from the early 4th century was found in 1955 at Berkasovo, Serbia, as part of the Berkasovo treasure; it is now in the Muzej Vojvodine (Museum of Vojvodina) in Novi Sad, Serbia. Although covered in glass jewels and possibly intended for ceremonial use, the helmet is made of iron and covered in silver gilt. It represents the style of helmet which was to predominate in 4th-century European warfare and beyond. Two more, slightly less decorated helmets were found with it. They are now designated Berkasovo I, II and III in terms of style (in accordance with earlier Roman helmet typologies). (Jebulon/Wikimedia/Public Domain)

LEFT
This Late Roman ridge helm is a 4th-century Berkasovo-type example, made of iron and covered in silver gilt; it was found in Deurne in the Netherlands. It is inscribed by a member of the *equites stablesiani*, cavalry *vexillationes* created by Gallienus (r. 253–68) in the late 3rd century and still listed in the *Notitia Dignitatum*, which has 15 such units stationed throughout the empire. It is quite possible that several units of the *equites stablesiani* faced the Goths between 376 and 378. The Deurne helmet and the Berkasovo types have cheek pieces which cover the ears; it has been argued that this feature means that they were cavalry helmets, while those that do not have such cheek pieces are argued to be infantry types. (Michiel/Wikimedia/CC BY-SA 2.0)

at Adrianople were greater, even though the Goths still outnumbered the Romans. Ammianus does tell us (31.7.16) that the site of the battle was still white with bones, possibly witnessed by him when he toured the fields on his way to Rome – although it is a literary trope stretching back to Tacitus (*Annals* 1.61). Libanius (*Oration 24*: 4) also mentions the piles of bones still visible on the field. Ammianus surmises (31.7.16) that the Romans suffered serious losses, as did the Goths. He further tells us that some men of distinction fell, although he does not name them; it is possible Profuturus was one. As far as the Romans were concerned the battle was a draw at best, although it did show that disciplined Roman troops could hold out against the Goths for an extended period.

Following the battle, the Romans retreated to the nearby city of Marcianopolis (Ammianus, 31.8.1) and the Goths retreated to their wagon laager, from which they did not stir for seven days. This implies that they had suffered in the battle. Seizing the opportunity, the Romans raised high barriers (*aggerum obiectu celsorum*) (Ammianus, 31.8.1) to confine the Goths in the Haemus Mountains, trapping them between there and the Danube. The Roman intention was, once again, to starve the Goths into submission. Meanwhile, Richomeres returned to Gaul (Ammianus, 31.8.2). Upon learning of the less than satisfactory outcome of the year's campaigning, Valens sent another commander, Saturninus, temporarily given command of the Roman cavalry as *magister equitum*, to render assistance to Profuturus and Traianus (Ammianus, 31.8.3).

The food supplies in Moesia Secunda and Scythia were exhausted and the Goths attempted to break through the Roman defences, but to no avail. They therefore entered into an alliance with some Huns and Halani, promising them booty. Saturninus gathered his forces together and prepared to retreat in case they were overrun. Ammianus states (31.8.5) that Saturninus' plan was not a foolish one, as the Goths might still overwhelm the Romans. As soon as the Romans retreated and the passes were open to the Goths, they burst out into Thrace, bringing devastation everywhere, reaching as far as the Hellespont and the Rhodope Mountains (Ammianus, 31.8.6).

Adrianople

9 August AD 378

BACKGROUND TO BATTLE

When the Goths burst out of the Haemus Mountains, they made their way to the town of Dibaltum (near modern-day Debelt, Bulgaria). There they found the Roman commander Barzimeres, a *tribunus* of the *scutarii* (Ammianus, 31.8.9), with the *Cornuti* and some infantry just as he was making camp. By *c.*395, the *Cornuti* – a cavalry unit of the *auxilia palatina* listed in the *Notitia Dignitatum* – were part of the troops commanded by the *magister peditum praesentalis* in the West and the *Cornuti iuniores* were part of the troops commanded by the *magister militum praesentalis* in the East. The Goths fell on Barzimeres, who charged but was surrounded by enemy cavalry – perhaps the Huns and the Halani (Ammianus, 31.8.3) – and was killed.

The Goths next sought out Frigiderius himself (Ammianus, 31.9.1), who had returned to Thrace on Gratian's advice. He was at Beroea, probably modern-day Veria in northern Greece. Ammianus praises Frigiderius (31.9.2) as knowing both how to command his soldiers and preserve them; learning of the Goths' approach, he withdrew into Illyricum. While withdrawing, his troops massed in *cuneus* formation, he came upon the Gothic chieftain Farnobius (who had crossed into the empire later in 376) leading his own men and his allies, the Taifali. Frigiderius was able to inflict a heavy defeat on this band and killed Farnobius, sparing those who were left and banishing them to work the fields of Italy (Ammianus, 31.9.4). This occurred just before the onset of winter in 377.

In the West, the Alemanni raided over the frontier, perhaps encouraged by news that Gratian was heading east to assist Valens. This distracted and delayed Gratian into 378 and would hold up his departure to assist his uncle, Valens. His eventual success against the Alemanni might also have played a part in helping Valens decide to fight the Goths alone at Adrianople.

OPPOSITE
This Roman *spatha*, found at the fort of Nigrum Pullum on the Rhine in what is now Zwammerdam in the Netherlands, dates from the later 3rd century (Provincie Zuid-Holland Inv. 28807). As the 3rd century progressed, the longer *spatha* was adopted by nearly all combatants and the shorter *gladius* fell out of use. (Provincie Zuid-Holland/ Wikimedia/CC BY 4.0)

The year 378 saw Valens finally depart from Antioch and march for Constantinople (Ammianus, 31.11.1). Socrates (4.38) mentions Valens entering Constantinople on 30 May, but being ridiculed by the people for inaction. As a result of these insults, Valens left the city on 11 June and advanced against the Goths. Sozomen also tells us (6.40) that the people were indignant at Valens' inaction, and demanded that they themselves be armed and be allowed to fight in their own defence. These accusations offended Valens and he immediately undertook his expedition against the Goths. This is probably also the context of a brief fragment of Eunapius' *Universal History* (F44.5), which tells us that a furious Valens ordered his whole army to move against the enemy.

We now hear in Ammianus that Traianus was relieved of his command of the infantry; this command was transferred to Sebastianus (31.11.1). Profuturus is not mentioned. Ammianus tells us (31.11.1) only that Sebastianus had been sent from Italy at his own request, whereas in Zosimus and Eunapius we find that he was slandered at the Western court by jealous eunuch-courtiers (Zosimus, 4.22.4). Zosimus tells us (4.22.4) that Valens despaired of the poor quality of his own commanders; this certainly fits with their performances in 376 and 377 but (according to Zosimus) Valens could not dismiss them in the circumstances of 378.

In such a context Sebastianus arrived from the West. Ammianus' account seems to combine elements from both a positive account of Sebastianus and a negative one, and he eventually comes down on the negative side. The purely positive version can still be gleaned from Eunapius and Zosimus. Not only does this provide a different perspective to Ammianus' in that case (a relatively rare occurrence), it also provides the grounds for giving credence to our other sources for the battle of Adrianople. Even though most of these other accounts are very brief, there are still elements of value to be found which add to or contrast with Ammianus' account. Juggling them all and trying to find a clear narrative becomes difficult, however, especially when they contradict our best and fullest account in Ammianus. Nevertheless, incorporating them into Ammianus' overall narrative makes for a richer and fuller picture.

A fragment of Eunapius' *Universal History* (F44.1) – not present in Zosimus' writings – warns that an army should not do battle with an enemy who despair for their lives and are ready to face any danger (as the Goths had shown at the battle of Marcianopolis). Instead, the war should be dragged out and they should be starved; a decisive battle should not be risked. This seems to support the policy Sebastianus would pursue, although he is not named in the fragment (but Zosimus does give similar arguments to him). F44.3 from the *Suda* (σ 177) records Eunapius' view of Sebastianus, claiming that he exceeded all expectations as a soldier because he possessed all the virtues. We are told that he loved war, but refused to take risks; he fits with the image of the ideal general going back to Hannibal. He cared for his men, but did not pander to them; he punished those who did not follow orders, but rewarded those who did. At the same time, he removed the desire for plunder from his forces. These are the tropes of the re-disciplining general going back to the Roman Republic. The fragment accords with the jealousy of eunuch-courtiers, which saw Sebastianus removed from his Western commands.

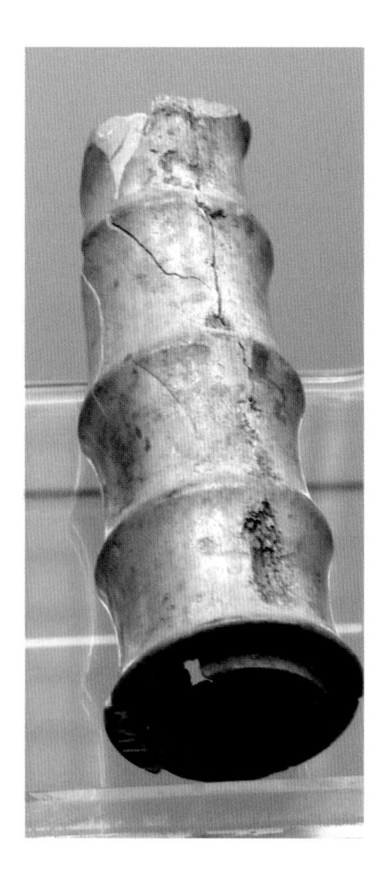

This 4th-century bone grip for a *spatha* is now in the Museum Lauriacum in Enns, Austria. (Wolfgang Sauber/ Wikimedia/CC BY-SA 3.0)

According to Ammianus (31.11.1), Sebastianus travelled to the imperial villa of Melanthius; this may have been a village between 102 and 140 *stadia* (19–26km) from Constantinople, according to other sources (the *Suda*, s.v. *Melantia*; Agathias, 5.14 D). There – and this seems to be the evidence of a negative tradition – Sebastianus tried to win the favour of the troops by paying them and giving them supplies. These hardly seem coercive acts, but probably reflect accounts which slandered Sebastianus. He then marched to Nice in Thrace; this could be a town or a *mansio* (an official stopping on a Roman road), according to Socrates (2.37.95), probably near modern-day Havsa, Turkey. There, Sebastianus learned that a band of Goths, weighed down with plunder, were near Adrianople and moving towards a permanent Gothic encampment near Beroea and Nicopolis (Ammianus, 31.11.2).

Sebastianus chose 300 men from each *legio* and marched rapidly by forced marches to Adrianople. Ammianus records (31.11.2) that Sebastianus was ordered to do this, so the directive may have come from Valens. This detail in Ammianus combined with Eunapius and Zosimus may give us a detail not recorded elsewhere. According to Zosimus (4.23.1), Sebastianus was appointed *magister militum* and given command for the whole war. He did not trust the discipline of the soldiers and commanders (Zosimus, 4.23.2), so he chose 2,000 men from the entire army to train and reform. With this force, Sebastianus secured the cities and launched ambushes against the Goths as they foraged (Zosimus, 4.23.4). If the 300 men from each *legio* amounted to 2,000 men in total, then it tells us that Sebastianus had approximately seven *legiones* with him. We can add this (minimum of) 7,000 men to the numbers of the army when joined by Valens. If Sebastianus' *legiones* were stronger than 1,000 men, we still arrive at seven *legiones*, but the number of men could differ depending on how many we accept per *legio*.

The detail of why the detachments of men were chosen is absent in Ammianus. Eunapius records (F44.4) that Sebastianus only asked for 2,000 men (see also Zosimus, 4.23.2), the motivation for the small number being that their success would inspire others to wish to join them. This certainly allows for the explanation found in Zosimus (4.23.2) that the other commanders at (the Eastern) court turned Valens against Sebastianus too, rather than Ammianus' view (31.12.6) that it was Sebastianus who encouraged the risky manoeuvre of the emperor himself offering open battle. Zosimus' account of Sebastianus gives us a sense of how much the author left out when using Eunapius' *Universal History* as his source.

When Sebastianus approached Adrianople, he was refused entry (Ammianus, 31.11.3) because the garrison thought he might have gone over to the side of the Goths and feared a stratagem. Sebastianus was, at last, recognized and allowed to enter. The following morning, he sallied against the Goths and caught up with them near the Hebrus River (the modern-day Maritsa/Meriç/Evos River, which runs through Bulgaria, Turkey and Greece respectively). There, Sebastianus set an ambush and fell on a Gothic band at night and destroyed almost all of their number (Ammianus, 31.11.4). News of this setback alarmed Fritigern, who was wary of Sebastianus (Ammianus, 31.11.5) and recalled his ravaging bands to him, near the town of Cabyle, to save them from attack. Fritigern then left the area.

Gratian wrote to Valens, informing the emperor of his victory over the Alemanni and telling him that he was on his way to assist him against the Goths (Ammianus, 31.11.6). Ammianus then tells us (31.12.1) that Valens was troubled by Gratian's success against the Alemanni. Zosimus relates (4.23.2) that because of jealousy of his successes, Sebastianus was slandered at the court of Valens, just as he had been in the West. Principal among these men was probably Traianus, who had been recalled to Valens' court and replaced by Sebastianus (Ammianus, 31.12.1).

Sebastianus cautioned Valens not to make open war on so numerous an opponent (Zosimus, 4.23.6), telling him that he should instead continue to conduct the ambushes and manoeuvres which he had undertaken so successfully. These were exactly the tactics Ammianus himself urged (31.7.2), but he gives Sebastianus no credit for recommending them. Sebastianus' opponents at Valens' court – the officers deprived of command by him and those not employed in his operations with such a small force – agitated against him, telling Valens that he should lead the army out and go to war (Zosimus, 4.24.1). They sought to encourage Valens by commenting that the Goths were almost completely destroyed and that victory would be easy. According to Zosimus (4.24), Valens followed their advice and led the army out, although this ties in with the accounts of agitation in the Hippodrome. By contrast, Ammianus states (31.12.1) that Sebastianus exaggerated his successes and that it was he who encouraged Valens to do battle without waiting for Gratian. It is possible that, because Sebastianus was among the fallen at the battle of Adrianople (Ammianus, 31.13.18), the sources Ammianus interviewed after the battle blamed Sebastianus, and took no responsibility themselves. Others have viewed Zosimus as being tainted in his support for Sebastianus, whose military career went back to the reign of Julian (r. 361–63).

Zosimus' summary of events of 377–78 is poor. He tells us (4.21) that Valens left Antioch and marched into Thrace via Constantinople, but there is nothing in his account concerning the attitude of the people there. We get some detail in Zosimus' comment (4.22.1) that Valens sent his Saracens, expert cavalry he had brought with him from the East, against the Goths. This corresponds to and corroborates with Ammianus' account (31.16.5), but according to Ammianus the Saracen raids occurred only after the battle of Adrianople. Zosimus tells us (4.21.2) that the Saracens caught and killed many Goths in small groups, but avoided larger contingents. Such tactics were similar to those of Sebastianus, but again he gets no credit. In Zosimus' account, it was these raids which caused the Goths to withdraw from around Constantinople, allowing Valens to bring his army into the field. This detail may tie in with the actions of Sebastianus, which caused the Gothic withdrawal and Fritigern to pull his marauding bands back to Cabyle. Whatever the truth, Valens now led out his army from Constantinople.

A 5th-century example of a *spatha* and scabbard furniture from the Alemanni (from the Upper Rhine). Gratian defeated the Alemanni shortly before moving to assist Valens at the battle of Adrianople; but his successes in battle may have spurred Valens to face the Goths alone. The *spatha* was ubiquitous as the sword of choice for both the Romans and their enemies throughout the 4th century. (Bullenwächter/Wikimedia/ CC BY-SA 3.0)

Adrianople, 9 August AD 378

MAP KEY

1 Marching over rough ground, Valens heads north with an army of 60,000 men, mostly infantry. Close to noon, he reaches the eighth milestone from Adrianople. The wagon laager of the Goths is spotted.

2 Valens deploys. The Roman cavalry (**A**) are deployed on the right, in front of the infantry. This contains the units of the *scholae palatini* known as the *schola scutariorum prima* (**B**), *schola scutariorum secunda* (**C**), *schola scutariorum sagittariorum* (**D**) and other cavalry units (**E**). After them, the infantry deploy; a mix of *legiones* and units of *auxilia* (**F**), with some skirmisher units in front (**G**). These units include the *lanciarii* (**H**) and *mattiarii* (**I**). Valens, with the *armigeri* and *candidati* (**J**) as bodyguards, is stationed on the right of the infantry formation. Other units, including the units of the *auxilia palatini* known as the *Batavi* (**K**), are positioned in a strong reserve (**L**). The Roman cavalry units which were to have made up the left wing of the Roman army have not made it to the battlefield.

3 Visible to the Romans is the Gothic wagon laager (**M**). Drawn up in front of it is a body of Gothic infantry (**N**) with archers behind as per usual (**O**). Unseen by the Romans, a larger unit of Gothic infantry (**P**) waits inside the wagon laager.

4 As the last of a series of envoys sent by the Goths to play for time returns to the Gothic lines, skirmishing by the cavalry units on the Roman right, the two units of *scutarii* and the *sagittarii*, escalates. The Roman cavalry are repulsed.

5 Smoke from fires lit deliberately by the Goths (**Q**) signals to the Gothic cavalry under Alatheus and Saphrax (**R**), including units of Halani, to charge from higher ground to the left of the wagon laager. The smoke partially obscures their advance.

6 The Roman cavalry on the right, already retreating, are taken by surprise by the Gothic cavalry. The Gothic cavalry charge home and send the Roman cavalry from the field.

7 The Gothic cavalry then surround the Roman infantry, firing missiles into them from all sides. The Romans nevertheless advance towards the Gothic wagon laager in a single body and crash into the infantry there. The Roman left wing manages to push the Goth infantry back to the wagon laager.

8 The Gothic cavalry force the Roman infantry together from right and left.

9 The Gothic infantry inside the wagon laager surge out and add to the Gothic forces surrounding the unprotected Roman infantry.

10 As the Roman forces begin to break at last, units (including the *Batavi* and *armigeri*) cut their way out and make their escape. The retreating Romans are cut down.

11 Valens, abandoned by the *armigeri*, makes his way with the remnants of his 40 *candidati*, to the *lanciarii* and *mattiarii*.

12 The Romans rout and are cut down as they flee. Valens is either killed fighting or makes his way, wounded, to a fortified farmhouse where he is burned alive by Goths pursuing the fleeing Romans.

Battlefield environment

Several locations for the battle of Adrianople have been suggested: north, north-east, and directly east of Adrianople itself. The first location lies north of the city between the Hebrus River (the modern-day Maritsa/Meriç/Evos River) to the west and the Tonzos/Tundzha River to the east. The second location also lies to the north, but further east, to the east of the Tonzos/Tundzha, near the modern-day Turkish town of Muratçali. A third location lies east of the city near the modern-day Turkish town of Demirhanlı (first proposed in 1903).

No consensus has been reached on the location of the battlefield, although there are several criteria which any site must meet – but, with the interpretation offered here, none of the currently proposed sites do. Sozomen wrote in his *Ecclesiastical History* (6.40) that the Goths retreated while being pursued and that the Romans found them encamped 'in a secure position' (*en asphalei chorio*), meaning on a hill. Sozomen is the only authority to give us this detail, but it seems a sound one – we are told that the Goths' wagon laager was on a hill before the battle of the Willows and that the Goths sought a hill to give impetus to their downward charge – and Sozomen's detail adds to our understanding of the battle. Lastly, Ammianus suggests that the returning Gothic cavalry rapidly descended from the mountains (31.12.17), telling us that there was higher ground close to the Gothic wagon laager from which the cavalry could charge. Most modern reconstructions of the battle have the Gothic cavalry charge from the Gothic right wing, but in this work I argue that they came from the left, so the higher ground should be sought there and not on the Gothic right. Using Ammianus and Hydatius, we can search for the site of the battlefield in a band 13–20km stretching north to east of Adrianople to fit these criteria. A dry plain on which the Goths lit their fires (Ammianus, 31.12.13) should also form part of the location of the battle.

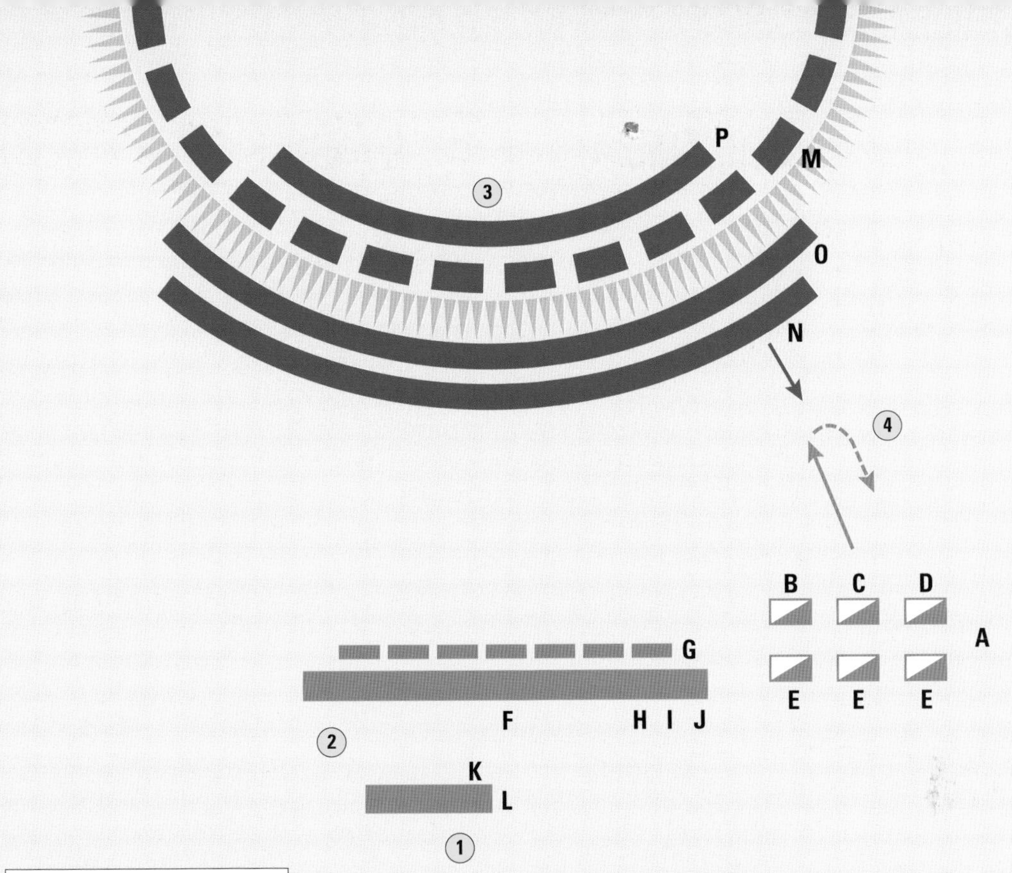
P
M
3
O
N
4
B
C
D
A
G
E
E
E
F
H
I
J
2
K
L
1
ADRIANOPLE: OPENING MOVES

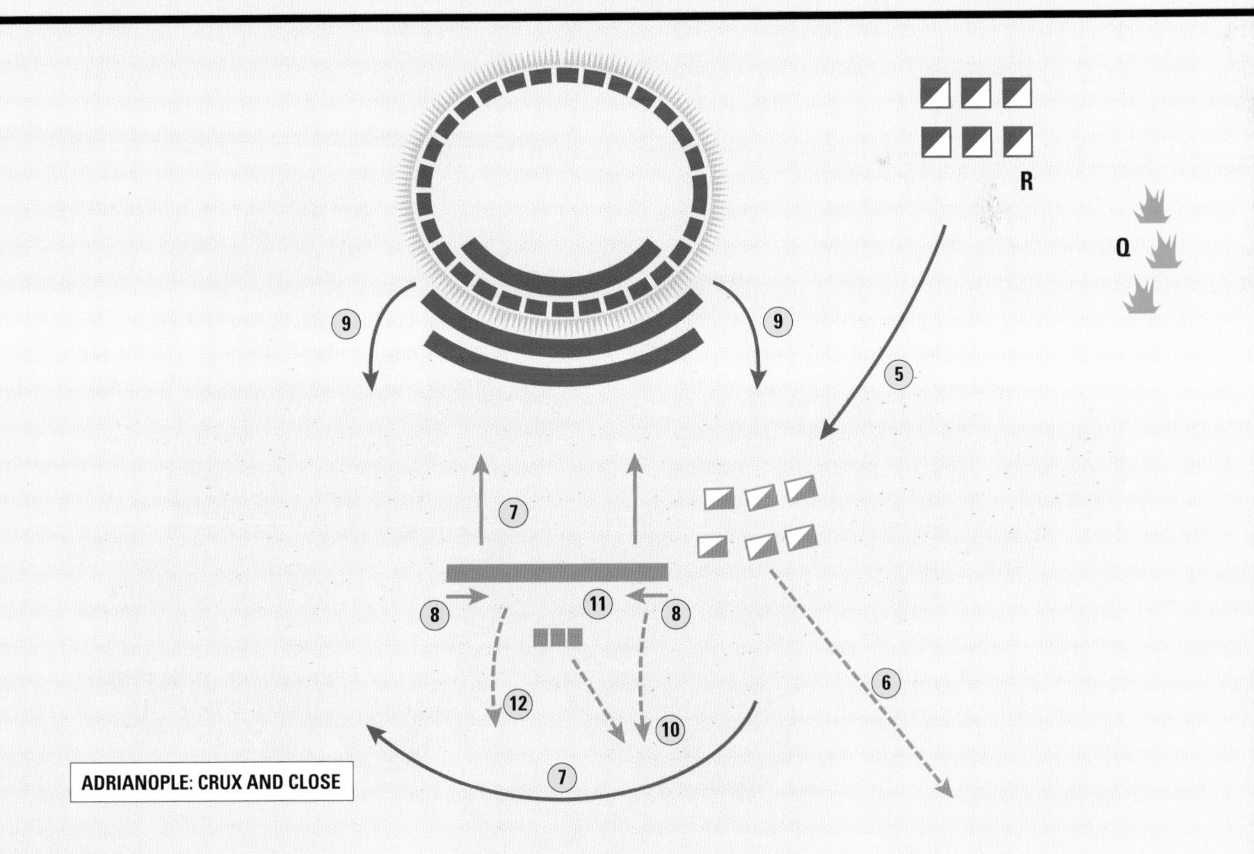
R
Q
9
9
5
7
8
11
8
6
12
10
7
ADRIANOPLE: CRUX AND CLOSE

INTO COMBAT

Ammianus tells us (31.12.1) that Valens marched from Melanthius, eager to perform some exploit equal to that of Gratian. Ammianus gives no detail of the army Valens took with him, only that it was numerous and was composed of different elements, including veterans and several men of high rank, such as Traianus. Valens' army probably consisted of parts of the *comitatus praesentalis* and the remaining units of the *comitatus* of Thrace, as well as the units of imperial *scholae*. Included in these may have been the remainder of Sebastianus' seven *legiones*, perhaps some of the Armenian *legiones* brought by Traianus and even some of the *limitanei* from Moesia Secunda and Scythia – all of which supports the idea of a large Roman force.

Roman scouts were sent out and units despatched to frustrate Gothic attempts to block the roads and disrupt the Roman supply line. These units included a *turma* ('squadron') of cavalry, perhaps only 30 men strong, and a unit of infantry archers (Ammianus, 31.12.2). The timings suggested in the account of Sozomen (6.40), who has Valens leaving Constantinople on 11 June, implies almost two months of manoeuvres before the battle. Ammianus also suggests the use of scouts and manoeuvres by both sides. According to Ammianus (31.12.3), for the next three days, the Goths advanced slowly over unfamiliar terrain until they were 24km from Constantinople and heading towards Nice. There they were spotted, and Valens was assured by his skirmishers that this body of Goths numbered only 10,000 men. Ammianus points out, however, that this was a mistake. Some commentators have taken this number to be the total number of Goths at Adrianople and have therefore placed low numbers at the battle, yet it seems clear that this number was only a portion of the Goths, not the whole nation on the move, and that the actual number was much greater. The incident also highlights the fact that

This 3rd-century Roman mail fragment is now in the Oberhausmuseum in Passau, Germany. The two most common armours were *squamata* (scales) and *hamata* (mail or chainmail). A limitation of surviving finds of Roman armour is that they can range from a single piece through to small sections. Very few full suits have been found and information must be gleaned from the surviving fragments. (Wolfgang Sauber/Wikimedia/CC BY-SA 3.0)

the reconnaissance of the Romans was, at best, incomplete and haphazard, especially if they had only found a portion of the Gothic force after three days of searching.

Learning that the Goths numbered 'only' 10,000 men, Valens determined to attack them himself at once (Ammianus, 31.12.3). Ammianus tells us (31.12.4) that Valens advanced in *agmine quadrato* ('battle array'), possibly a square formation, and made his way towards Adrianople. This organized advance is contradicted by other accounts, however. At Adrianople, Valens made a strong camp and 'impatiently' (Ammianus, 31.12.4) waited for Gratian. Richomeres, the Western *comes domesticorum*, arrived from Gratian once again, no doubt bringing troops from the *protectores* and *protectores domestici*, although no mention is made of them being understrength this time; perhaps with any threats in the West dealt with, it was his entire command. Richomeres also brought a letter from Gratian stating that he would soon arrive.

Valens called a council of his commanders (Ammianus, 31.12.5) and doubtless sought reassurance that he should attack alone so that he would not have to share the glory with his nephew. Ammianus (31.12.6) blames these advisors, influenced by Sebastianus, for encouraging Valens to fight alone and at once. As we have seen, Ammianus' portrayal of Sebastianus appears to make him the scapegoat for the defeat. Ammianus tells us (31.12.6) that Victor – the *magister equitum* and a slow and careful Sarmatian – recommended waiting for Gratian, as did many others. According to Ammianus (31.12.7), Valens insisted on fighting alone, which suggests that the meeting was arranged simply to approve the emperor's decision. According to Ammianus (31.12.7), Valens' decision to fight was evidence of his obstinacy, supported by the flatterers at court. The idea that some leading figures in Valens' command team opposed such a decision may have come with hindsight, especially as Sebastianus also opposed Valens fighting alone in the version of events presented by Eunapius (F44.3–4) and Zosimus (4.23.6–4.24.1). Are we to believe then that no one approved of Valens' plan? Victor survived the battle, as did Richomeres and Saturninus, and there may have been a deliberate move to blame those who had died, especially the two highest-ranking losses, Sebastianus and Traianus. Theodoret (4.33.2) assigns responsibility to Traianus after the Roman defeat at the battle of the Willows too, and it is possible that blame came directly from Valens.

Preparations for Valens' advance began, but at this moment a Christian presbyter arrived from Fritigern (Ammianus, 31.12.8), sent as an envoy to discuss peace. This was the first of several envoys sent by Fritigern and they have been accepted at face value by historians who have researched the battle. It is possible, though, that Fritigern was playing for time and using the envoys to enact some kind of premeditated plan. This is certainly in keeping with the description of Fritigern elsewhere as cunning and crafty (Ammianus, 31.5.4, 31.5.7, 31.12.14 & 31.16.3; Jordanes, 136), yet no modern commentator has discerned a deliberate Gothic stratagem at play at Adrianople. Ammianus even tells us (31.12.9) that Fritigern was crafty and deceitful, but no ancient account or modern reconstruction of the battle has considered that Valens played into Fritigern's hands. This is despite that fact that Ammianus records (31.15.7–9) other Gothic stratagems – probably Fritigern's initiatives – in the

Two views of a single Roman scale, showing the six holes used to attach the scales to each other and to the backing fabric on a suit of *squamata* (scale mail). It is tongue-shaped, flat, measures 35×19×1mm and weighs 1g. Although there is some variety in the shapes of scales and the number of holes on different suits – presumably manufactured at different *fabricae* around the empire – they achieve the same effect. This example was found in Darlington, England, and is made from copper alloy; it is part of the Portable Antiquities Scheme. (Philippa Walton/Wikimedia/CC BY 2.0)

Here we see two soldiers from the Great Hunt mosaic wearing decorated long-sleeved tunics (a style sometimes called the *tunica manicata*) and cloaks. The shield is decorated and the men have hunting spears, which appear to be shorter than military spears. They do not wear swords. Note the leggings and footwear and the central grip of the shield on the right. (Robur.q/ Wikimedia/CC BY-SA 3.0)

Consularia Constantinopolitana entry for the year 378, and on another occasion when the Romans expected a Gothic trick that did not materialize (31.7.5).

Fritigern's envoy came to the Roman camp and presented a letter requesting that the Goths be given Thrace, and all its crops and flocks, as land to occupy. If this request was granted, the Goths promised 'perpetual peace' (Ammianus, 31.12.8). At the same time, a secret letter was delivered, in which Fritigern claimed to look forward to being Valens' friend and ally – Ammianus claims (31.12.9) this was a pretence – but that he, Fritigern, could not control the ferocity of his people unless the emperor, on occasion, showed them an army close at hand. This seems to be a ploy of Fritigern's to persuade Valens to bring his army towards the Gothic wagon laager, perhaps because the Gothic leader had a stratagem in mind. The letter claimed that such an act by Valens would frighten the Goths into submission. Ammianus tells us (31.12.10) that the envoy was dismissed and looked on with suspicion by Valens, yet the Roman army set out on the following morning, 9 August. The Roman force left all of its baggage near Adrianople with a suitable guard of perhaps more than one *legio*; this implies that Valens believed he had more men at his disposal than he deemed necessary. The treasury, the praetorian prefect and the emperor's council stayed inside Adrianople.

Valens marched over rough ground towards the Goths in the heat of the late morning. Ammianus tells us (31.12.11) that Valens advanced *octavo* – 'eighth' – but eighth what? Some editors have chosen to emend this to *octavo hora*, so it reads 'eighth hour', or about 2.00pm. This, however, contradicts

Ammianus' 'towards noon' in the same sentence (31.12.11). What is more, there is no reason for the emendation and the *octavo* seems to be one of distance, not time, suggesting that Ammianus meant the eighth milestone from Adrianople. The entry for 378 in Hydatius' *Chronicle* refers to a distance of 12 Roman miles (18km) from Adrianople. This gives modern scholars a band of almost 13–20km from Adrianople for Valens' march, in an arc from north to east, to look for the battle site itself. That search has been ongoing for more than a century and there are still several candidates, each with reasons to accept and reject them.

At a distance of 13km (or 20km) from the city, the Romans saw the wagon laager of the Goths. The scouts reported that it was circular (literally 'turned by a lathe' – Ammianus, 31.12.11). The Goths uttered a fierce shout (Ammianus, 31.12.11) and the Roman officers marshalled their line. Ammianus then offers a detail (31.12.11) that is important for interpreting the events of the battle: the right wing of the Roman cavalry was placed in front and the greater part of the infantry behind – *subsidebat*, usually interpreted as 'in reserve' although it could mean 'in support'. A strong reserve had saved the day for the Roman forces at the battle of the Willows, so perhaps such a tactic was adopted again for that reason.

Ammianus tells us (31.12.12) that the cavalry of the Roman left wing was not present. They had been organized with difficulty and were still travelling to the battlefield while the army was deploying. The other surviving sources offer help here. Sozomen tells us (6.40) that Valens decided to attack before his men were in the proper order, while Socrates states (4.38) that the Roman cavalry revolted and refused to engage; whether this was the right wing or the left wing is unclear, but it was probably the cavalry who did not make it on

In addition to details of clothing, the Great Hunt mosaic also reveals details of horse trappings and a variety of shields. Despite the variety – and bearing in mind the limitations of pre-industrialized manufacture – the shields seem to be of a uniform design and dimensions, circular or perhaps oval with a central boss. This conforms with the designs reproduced in the *Notitia Dignitatum* from the late 4th or early 5th centuries and other sources, such as the *missoria* of both Valentinian I and Theodosius I. (DEA/ ARCHIVIO J. LANGE/Getty Images)

to the battlefield. Zosimus' brief account of the battle of Adrianople (4.24.1–2) – he probably did not take advantage of a larger account in Eunapius' *Universal History* – also adds to this picture. We are told that Valens led his whole army against the Goths in complete disarray; the 'barbarians' met them without hesitation and won an easy victory, almost totally annihilating the Romans. In Ammianus' summation of Valens (31.14.5), the author states that the emperor was untrained in the art of war, a claim which certainly seems borne out in the Adrianople campaign.

Ammianus then tells us (31.12.12) that the 'barbarians' were terrified by the clashing of Roman weapons and shields. Some of the Goths must therefore have been drawn up in front of their wagon laager – perhaps the 10,000 cited earlier. This terror was because part of the Gothic forces, namely the cavalry under Alatheus and Saphrax, was far away (Ammianus, 31.12.12) and, though sent for, had not yet arrived. This may, however, have been what Fritigern and the Goths wanted the Romans to think because when the Gothic cavalry did return, they returned *en masse*, and at the exact moment to deliver a decisive cavalry charge. It is clear that the Romans had no idea where the Gothic cavalry were. It seems more likely that the Gothic cavalry were getting into position to deliver just such a charge and that Fritigern was playing for time. The 'terror' of his men was exactly in accord with what Fritigern told Valens would happen when a Roman army appeared to bring the Goths back into line – and more envoys would soon follow.

Most modern reconstructions of the battle have the Gothic cavalry away foraging (so not in a single body) but it still managed to return, organize and deliver its decisive charge at the precise moment required for a Gothic victory. Modern reconstructions of the battle also accept that the Goths were actually terrified even though they had defeated successive Roman armies – the victorious Gothic commanders were present at Adrianople – and they probably still outnumbered the Roman army brought against them. Perhaps, if a smaller part of the Gothic forces was drawn up outside the wagon laager, these troops played their part in enticing the Romans to attack (uphill) by their feigned terror, and their small numbers made the Romans confident of success. The Romans may even have believed that they outnumbered the Goths, which might explain Roman confidence and why skirmishing on the Roman right began the battle.

Fritigern's playing for time is reinforced by his next action: to send more envoys suing for peace. The first envoys sent were of low birth, however, and were rejected by Valens (Ammianus, 31.12.13), who demanded that higher-ranking men be sent. Ammianus recognizes here that these envoys were playing for time, but argues that such a ploy was simply to allow time for the Gothic cavalry to return, not get into a position behind and above the Gothic wagon laager – a position that the Romans could not have reconnoitred.

Ammianus then includes a detail (31.12.13) which modern reconstructions of the battle have not made much of: that in addition to the heat of an early August day, which parched the Romans' throats, they were also suffering from the smoke generated by fires burning on the plain – fires deliberately lit by the Goths. Ammianus' explanation is that these fires were intended to exacerbate the thirst of the Romans. The fires may also have been a signal to the Gothic cavalry to return, or perhaps the smoke generated was intended to conceal their descent from higher ground (or both). We are told earlier of Gothic signalling, although it is unclear what these signals were; they are usually interpreted as the sound of war-trumpets (Ammianus, 31.5.8), but they could have been fire signals, as Gibbon (1776: 1056) believed. Some modern reconstructions of the battle assert that the flames were the result of grass fires and see no subterfuge in Fritigern's sending of envoys, but this does not seem to be the case. There are also many later references to the battle making use of a flame analogy (Libanius, *Oration 24*: 3–5; Themistius, *Oration 16*: 206d–207a), which seems to suggest that flames did indeed play a part in the battle – perhaps a more important part than Ammianus lets on. Fire was also to be used as a signal in the Goths' plan to take the city of Adrianople (Ammianus, 31.15.8).

This Late Roman military belt buckle dates from the 4th or 5th centuries. Military belts had long been symbols of status in the Roman Army; in the 4th century, highly decorated belts were worn by officers and any who could afford such decoration. (Arne Hodalic/Corbis via Getty Images)

Crafty Fritigern (Ammianus, 31.12.14) then sent a common soldier as a herald to request that the Romans send men of noble rank as hostages to him and he would withstand the anger of his men (the phrase is unclear, but seems to relate to the idea of negotiating or declaring peace). This was a ploy, however, to play for more time. Argument among the Romans over who should go took more time (Ammianus, 31.12.15); the *tribunus* Aequitius – a relative of Valens and the *cura palatii*, in charge of the palace – was chosen but he objected, arguing that he had been captured at the battle of Dibaltum but had escaped, a detail not mentioned in Ammianus' account of that battle (31.8.9–10). Ammianus' placing of Aequitius at Dibaltum implies that the battle may have been a more significant loss than his brief account earlier suggests.

Richomeres then volunteered to represent the Romans, and began to make his way to the Gothic wagon laager (Ammianus, 31.12.15). When Richomeres was on his way, however, he was prevented from completing his journey because, while the wrangling over who would go as a hostage to the Goths was taking place, the *sagittarii* and *scutarii* – led by Baccurius of Iberia (in Armenia) and Cassio – stationed on the Roman right wing rushed forward and engaged the Goths (Ammianus, 31.12.16). We are told that the *sagittarii* and *scutarii* attacked too rashly and were then put to flight. Skirmishing often escalated into battle in the later 4th century (Ammianus 27.10.10, 28.5.5–6 & 31.12.16; *cf.* 14.2.17) so there is every reason to accept that this sequence of events happened at Adrianople too, perhaps deliberately encouraged by the Goths.

In most modern interpretations of the battle of Adrianople, the *sagittarii* and *scutarii* have been viewed as infantry units, literally archers and shield-men akin to targeteers; the peltasts of Greek warfare were identified by their shields. MacDowall (2001: 73) seems to have been the first to suggest that the *sagittarii* and *scutarii* engaged on the Roman right could have been cavalry units – followed by Donnelly (2013) and Coombs-Hoar (2015) – and identified them with units mentioned in the *Notitia Dignitatum*. All the evidence for such an interpretation is, however, in Ammianus (and corroborated by diverse sources) and it makes (more) sense of Ammianus' account. The *sagittarii* and *scutarii* could therefore have been two specifically named units of the *scholae*.

The *Notitia Dignitatum* (23.2–6) names the seven units of *scholae* serving the Eastern Roman Emperor in *c.*390, under the command of the *Magister Officiorum* (Master of Offices). Only in the East were there units of *scholae* named the *schola scutariorum prima* (23.2), *schola scutariorum secunda* (23.3) and *schola scutariorum sagittariorum* (23.5). It is possible that the titles of these units had become honorific and no longer referred to their battlefield role (and describing units with shields (*scuta*) seems redundant). If these units are the *scutarii* and *sagittarii* of Ammianus (31.12.16), however, then the course of the battle of Adrianople actually becomes clearer: on the Roman right, the cavalry, already ahead of the deploying infantry units (Ammianus, 31.12.11), became engaged with the Gothic left, perhaps provoked into doing so by the howls of the Goths or deliberate skirmishing to make them engage. This interpretation does, however, re-write the battle entirely in terms of modern reconstructions and how the battle fits into subsequent military history. Elsewhere, Ammianus refers colloquially to *scholae* units: during his account of Constantius II's (r. 337–61) entry into Rome in 357 (16.10.8), he refers to the *schola scutariorum clibanariorum* (*Notitia Dignitatum*, 23.6) simply as *cataphractarii* and *clibanarii* (units of heavily armoured cavalry); and only a few chapters before his account of the battle of Adrianople he refers to the *Cornuti* (31.8.9) rather than the *Cornuti seniores* or *Cornuti iuniores*. Therefore, Ammianus' mentions of *scutarii* and *sagittarii* may represent references to the two (or more) *scholae* units.

The Roman cavalry were repulsed and their retreat was followed immediately by the charge of the Gothic cavalry under Alatheus and Saphrax, combined with a group of Halani (Ammianus, 31.12.17). Ammianus' turn of phrase makes clear that the appearance of the Gothic cavalry was a shock – they appeared like a thunderbolt from the mountains, spreading slaughter among all they came across, perhaps implying that they charged from higher ground. If the Roman units were indeed cavalry and withdrawing or retreating already, then the charge of the Gothic cavalry would most assuredly have been into them to take advantage of their setback. Again, most modern reconstructions of the battle have shown the Gothic cavalry charging into the Roman left, where there was no cavalry, but the charge of the Gothic cavalry into the retreating and disordered Roman cavalry on the right makes the most sense. Some modern authors, such as Wolfram (2005: 127), have argued that the Gothic charge was into the Roman right, while others have split the Gothic cavalry into a left and a right, for they seem to have appeared later in the battle on the Roman left too, but this was after they had surrounded the Roman infantry. For the Gothic cavalry to deliver such a decisive charge at precisely the right moment, they needed to have got into the ideal position. The envoys, the (signal) fires and the deliberately provoked skirmishing on the Roman right wing all seem to suggest that this was Fritigern's plan all along, tricking the Romans into an engagement whereby he could deliver a decisive blow. Combined with his request the day before that Valens approach the Goths and show himself at the head of an armed host, these insights seem to paint a very different picture of the battle.

The total defeat of the Roman cavalry on the right, suggested by Ammianus' criticisms (31.12.16), would have meant that Valens' forces were indeed left without any cavalry on the field at all, and the infantry could have

Ammianus includes details of war-cries on both sides and of musical instruments. Here we see the curved *cornu* being used by the *cornicen*, the junior officer who played it. The personnel shown here wear the same tunic and leggings as the other contemporary soldiers depicted on the Arch of Constantine. The man behind the musician bears a shield with an off-centre grip and seems to carry a *plumbata*, the fletched missile used by 4th- and 5th-century Roman infantry. (DEA/ARCHIVIO J. LANGE/Getty Images)

been surrounded by the Gothic forces. The Roman cavalry took no further part in the battle (horses being trampled are mentioned), and other accounts refer to the absence of protecting cavalry. If this interpretation is correct, Ammianus has, in fact, told us the fate of the Roman cavalry all along. We should remember that around 20 per cent of the Roman army at the battle of Adrianople may have consisted of cavalry units, a proportion which the two (or three) named units of *scutarii* and *sagittarii* alone cannot account for. The other cavalry units may have been on the Roman right as well and the Gothic cavalry charge caused them to flee also.

Orosius' account of the battle seems to confirm this interpretation; he states (7.33.13) that it was a war full of tears (meaning many Roman dead) against Goths now well prepared with a trained army and abundant resources. As soon as the *turmae* of the Roman cavalry were thrown into confusion by the sudden attack of the Goths, they left the companies of infantrymen without protection. Orosius goes on to tell us (7.33.14) that the Gothic cavalry surrounded the Roman *legiones* on all sides (*undique*) and overwhelmed them with clouds of arrows. The Romans, mad with fear, were driven over treacherous ground and completely cut to pieces by Gothic blades. As the only Roman cavalry on the field were those on the right, this mounted contingent must have been that which was unexpectedly attacked, and the reference to an unexpected attack makes most sense if it relates to the attack made by the Gothic cavalry, as the Romans did not know where the enemy horsemen were.

The *Chronicon* (or *Chronicle*) of Jerome was written in 380 as a continuation of the *Chronicle* of Eusebius of Caesarea. It is therefore one

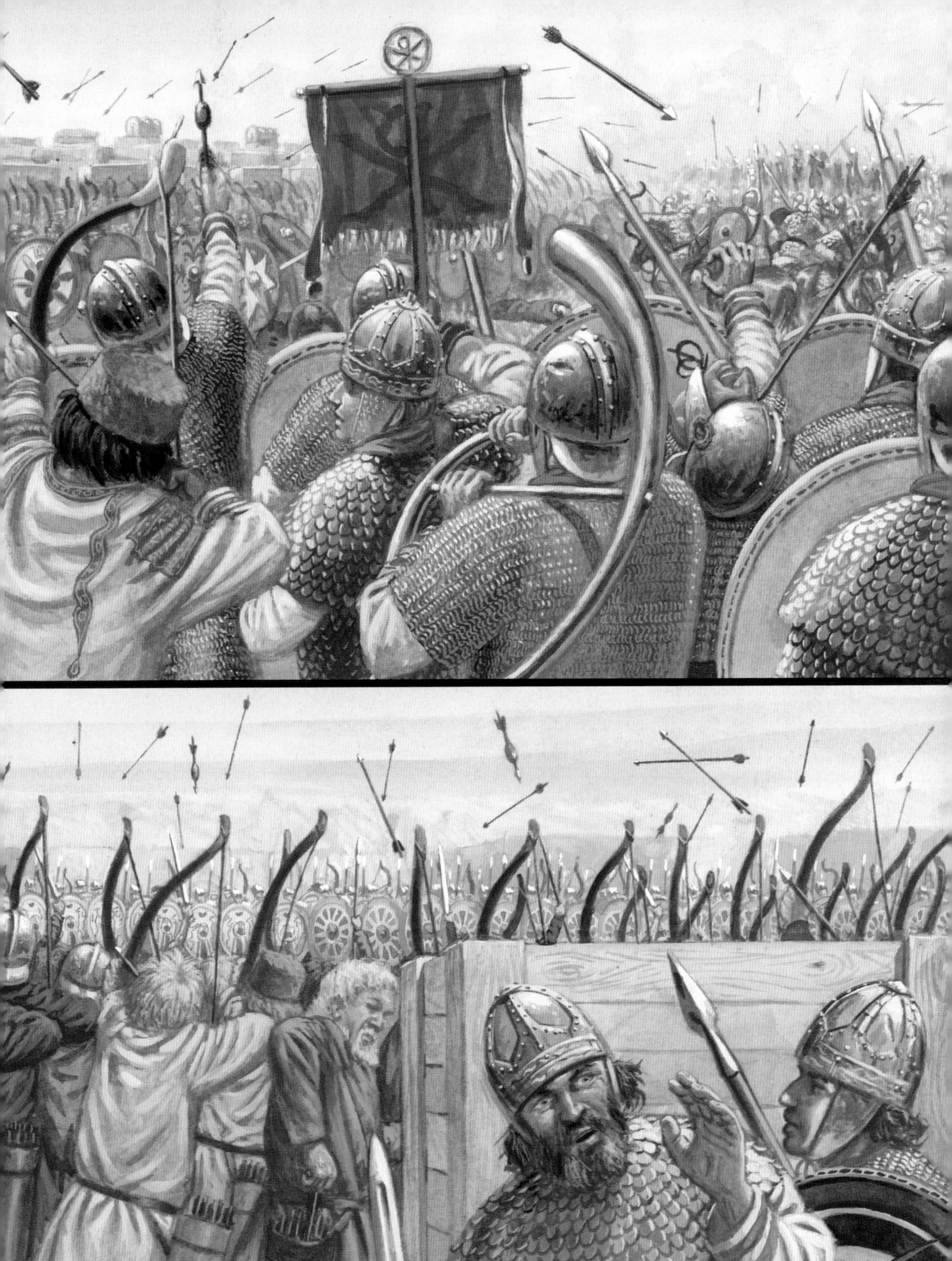

Adrianople

Roman view: From within the ranks of the unit of *mattiarii* (Ammianus, 31.13.8), the Romans advance uphill towards the Gothic wagon laager. In front of the wagon laager is a line of Gothic infantry and behind them, archers. Some of the Roman archers fire back; other Roman troops, armed with *plumbatae*, throw their missiles as they advance. The Romans wear a variety of scale and mail armours and helmets. Some seem to have gone into battle wearing Pannonian hats and tunics; a complaint soon after the battle – and stated as one of the reasons for the defeat – was that Roman soldiers had become accustomed to eschewing armour and helmets in combat. On the Roman right, the units which started the battle – the cavalry units of the *scutarii* and the *sagittarii* – are already in retreat, having advanced impetuously only to be repulsed. The Gothic cavalry, arriving unexpectedly and partially obscured by smoke, pursue the fleeing Roman cavalry; they will soon run them off the battlefield and surround the Roman infantry, cutting them down with incessant archery and javelin volleys.

Gothic view: From within the first line of wagons of the Gothic wagon laager, hidden reinforcements await the optimal moment to burst forth and overwhelm the advancing Roman infantry. Just in front of the wagons is the line of Gothic warriors and archers who wear and use a combination of their own equipment and that plundered from various Roman units over the previous two years. Even so, some Goths remain unarmoured and bareheaded, but are still prepared to display their personal bravery to their chiefs and fellow warriors. The large number of Gothic archers creates problems for the Romans, who must get into hand-to-hand combat range to have a chance of winning the battle. On the Gothic left, the Roman cavalry units retire; the charge of their own Gothic and Halani cavalry will signal the moment for the Gothic infantry reinforcements to emerge and add to the destruction of the Roman infantry, charging the *mattiarii* in front of them, the *labarum* and *cornicen* (a junior officer who provided signals in battle via the *cornu*, a wind instrument) providing a focal point for their attack. Next to the *mattiarii*, men of the *lanciarii* advance.

of our earliest historical sources for the battle. Nevertheless it is very brief. The penultimate entry covers the battle of Adrianople, but there is insight within it. Jerome surmises (331c) that the Roman *legiones* were surrounded and lacked the protection of horse and were consequently slaughtered. This can be seen to add weight to Ammianus' account (although the 'surrounded' is explicit) and to Orosius' account at 7.33.14. The judgement that the *legiones* lacked the protection of cavalry on the flanks is also adroit, not only on the left where the Roman horsemen did not arrive, but also on the right where the Roman cavalry were driven off by the Gothic and Halani cavalry. Sozomen also tells us (6.40) that the Roman cavalry was dispersed, his tiny detail adding to the overall picture.

The battle was not over, however, as the Roman infantry were still intact, albeit surrounded by Gothic cavalry; they now advanced (Ammianus, 31.13.1). The Romans sounded their war-trumpets and this, along with the bellowing of officers, rallied the troops. Ammianus states (31.13.1) that the battle spread like flames and that the Romans were assailed by javelins and arrows (from both Gothic infantry and cavalry). Ammianus mixes his metaphors – in the next line he remarks that the two lines (of infantry) dashed against each other like the rams of ships and the lines were tossed like waves at sea (31.13.2). The Roman left wing had advanced all the way to the Gothic wagon laager; at this point, Ammianus tells us (31.13.2), they were deserted by the remainder of the Roman cavalry (perhaps those *vexillationes* not stationed on the right) and were therefore hard-pressed by the enemy's numbers, and crushed together. Now unprotected, the Roman infantry crowded together so close that soldiers could barely draw their swords. Added to this, great clouds of dust arose and the missiles of the Goths (Ammianus, 31.13.2) – once more telling us that the Romans were by now surrounded – could not be seen coming.

Now, Ammianus adds (31.13.3), the 'barbarians' rushed out with their enormous host. This seems to imply that more Goths were hidden inside the wagon laager and that the troops drawn up outside it were sufficiently numerous to entice the Romans to engage, but that more troops waited inside the ring of wagons, perhaps to add more arrows to the hail of missiles assailing the Romans. Some modern reconstructions of the battle place more Gothic infantry behind the wagon laager, but this is unnecessary. Fritigern, it seems, had more than one trick up his sleeve. This new surge of Goths left no room for retreat for the Romans, who fought to the last (Ammianus, 31.13.3).

We also get a clue that Roman cavalry units were intermingled with the infantry units in the army – or perhaps some of the fleeing cavalry moved towards the infantry rather than away from the field. Ammianus tells us (31.1.3) that the charge of the Goths trampled men and horses; helmets and armour were split by axe-blows from both sides. At length, the Roman infantry had broken most of their spears and were forced to fight with swords; seeing no chance of escape, they plunged into the enemy ranks to sell their lives as dearly as they could (Ammianus, 31.13.5). The ground was soon slippery with blood (Ammianus, 31.13.6), but the sun was just reaching its zenith and the Romans fought on, hungry, thirsty and exhausted by the weight of their armour. Finally, Ammianus tells us (31.13.7), the Roman line was broken and those Romans who were left fled as best they could over unknown paths (31.13.8). This agrees with the brief account given by Orosius (7.33.14).

Valens was in the middle of this action, according to Ammianus (31.13.8), and he took refuge with two units, the *lanciarii* and the *mattiarii*. No one has yet suggested that the *mattiarii* relate to the *mattiobarbuli* of Vegetius (1.17), which would make them *plumbatae* troops. These two units had been paired earlier, in 361 (Ammianus, 21.13.16) and now, at Adrianople, they stood firm to the last. Valens was forced to this extremity because he was abandoned by his *armigeri* bodyguard. Traianus, seeing the emperor, urged his foreign auxiliaries to protect him. Hearing this, the *comes* Victor moved to bring the *Batavi* (probably a unit of *auxilia palatini*) to the emperor's aid, but he could not find any of them. He therefore made his escape; Richomeres and Saturninus also escaped (Ammianus, 31.13.9).

Only a moonless night saved the Romans from greater losses (Ammianus, 31.13.11). According to Ammianus (31.13.12), Valens was wounded by an arrow just as night was coming down but, the emperor having fought amid the common soldiers, his body was not identified. This was, however, only one of a plethora of stories relating to Valens' demise – even Ammianus provides two. The second version (Ammianus, 31.13.14–15) states that after Valens was wounded, he was taken to a fortified cottage by some of his bodyguard, the *candidati militares*, and a few eunuch-courtiers. Surrounded by the enemy, the occupants defended themselves whereupon the Goths piled wood and straw around the house and burned it and everyone in it, including the emperor. Ammianus says he knew this because one of the *candidati* leapt from the second-storey window, escaped the Goths and told the story.

Other than the emperor, Rome lost Traianus and Sebastianus, both men bearing the high rank of *magister militum*, as well as 35 *tribuni*, the commanders of several *numeri* – groups of troops that were not *legiones* or *auxilia* – Valerianus (in charge of the royal stables), Aequitius and Potentius, *tribunus* of the *promoti*, a select body of troops. Ursicinus, the former commander-in-chief, also died. All of these losses suggest that the Roman army was indeed sizeable, with many units; barely one-third of it survived. Ammianus concludes his account (31.13.19) by stating that Rome had not suffered such a massacre as the one at Adrianople since Cannae in 216 BC. According to Polybius (50.3), the Roman losses at Cannae were 70,000 infantry and 5,600 cavalry; Livy (22.49) records slightly fewer losses – 2,700 cavalry and 40,000 infantry. Somewhat enigmatically, Ammianus does state (31.13.19) that the Romans were deceived by trickery, but does not credit such ploys to Fritigern but rather to ill-fortune.

The impact of the Roman defeat was massive and would be felt until the Western Roman Empire fell, if indeed it was not one its leading causes. By comparing the battle of Adrianople to the battle of Cannae, Ammianus joined a contemporary chorus which recognized the loss at Adrianople as one of the greatest defeats Rome had ever suffered. Ammianus and several other historians (such as Jerome and Eunapius) ended their works with the calamity of Adrianople. The idea they wished to convey was that it was a seismic disaster, an interpretation accepted for many years, although recent historians have tended to downplay the importance of the battle. It would seem, however, that Adrianople was indeed a disaster and that assessments of the defeat as a key factor in the Western Roman Empire's downfall are closer to the mark than those which downplay the battle altogether.

Valens' death took on a greater importance in contemporary and later history not only because of the calamity of the battle, but because of the fact that Valens was an Arian Christian, considered by Nicene Christians (most of our Christian authors were Nicene Christians) to be a member of a heretical faction. There is little of this in the account offered by Ammianus (a traditional Hellenist), but the great variety of stories about the emperor's death also reveal that there were many differing accounts of the battle which circulated but which now are lost.

A bust of either Valens or the Western Roman Emperor Honorius now in the Musei Capitolini (Inv. MC494) in Rome. Valens met his death at the battle of Adrianople, either on the battlefield or in a fortified farmhouse afterwards. He chose to do battle with the Goths alone despite the fact that Gratian was en route to aid him. It is possible that Gratian's successes spurred Valens on, although it is also possible that Valens was the victim of Fritigern's cunning. (Jastrow/ Wikimedia/Public Domain)

Unsurprisingly, Ammianus writes very little concerning the religious beliefs of the emperor or the Goths. Framing the defeat of Valens at Adrianople in terms of his Arian faith, Jordanes' summary of the battle itself is brief indeed: 'a grievous battle took place and the Goths prevailed' (138). Jordanes views the loss, and Valens' being burned to death, as punishments for Valens leading the Goths away from the true (Nicene) faith and into the heresy of Arianism. Orosius writes (7.33.9) of the church being hacked apart by Valens and later characterizes the emperor's death as divine vengeance (7.33.15). Unlike those church historians who would have Valens play the coward, Socrates (4.38) mentions the story of the emperor being burned to death in a village, but instead asserts that he took off his imperial robe before plunging into the depths of the Roman infantry, there to meet his fate in their midst; Valens' body could not be recognized because he wore no identifying clothing.

Theodoret also remarks (4.32) that Valens paid the price of his impiety, but he does not even place Valens at the battle, instead claiming that the emperor stayed at a hamlet where he became trapped and was burned alive. In his brief summary of the battle, Theodoret comments (4.32) that the Romans could not stand against the Goths' charge, but turned tail and were slain as they fled. Jerome (331c) has a wounded Valens almost fall from his horse before taking refuge in a farm cottage, which was then burned by the pursuing Goths.

Sozomen tells us (6.40) that Valens decided to attack before his men were in the proper order. In the battle, the cavalry was dispersed, the infantry forced to retreat, and Valens dismounted and took refuge in a 'tower'; there he was burned to death. Surprisingly, Sozomen does not blame Valens' fate on his faith, despite the author's opposition to Arianism, evident elsewhere in his writings. Even Ammianus includes predictions about Valens' death by fire (31.1.2), stating that a Christian ascetic, Isaac, predicted that if Valens did not end the conflict between Arian and Nicene, he would lose the battle and be burned alive. Valens' fiery fate is also recorded by Theodoret (4.32.1–3) and Sozomen (6.40), who also mentions the ascetic Isaac. The surviving generals Victor and Saturninus had witnessed this prediction and after the battle, had Isaac freed from prison; Saturninus gave Isaac land which became the site of the first monastery in Constantinople.

At the same time as all of these Christian accounts of Valens receiving a suitable punishment for his heresy, we find that pagan writers viewed the battle in the exact same light. Eunapius of Sardis' surviving work is the *Vitae Sophistarum* (*Lives of the Sophists*). In it (480) he states that the battle was fierce and Valens' death 'strange'; the emperor's demise was, however, divine retribution for Valens having ordered the pagan philosopher Maximus of Ephesus to be put to death in 372. Just like the many accounts of Christian priests, Maximus had predicted that such a fate would befall the emperor, by which Valens' body would not be found and he would not be granted a tomb. Eunapius directs (480) the reader to his *Universal History*, in which he tells us he has dealt with the issue at length. Unfortunately, Zosimus only excerpted the barest narrative at this point and no other fragments tell us what further details Eunapius may have related. Zosimus states (4.24.2) simply that Valens and a few followers retreated to an unwalled village, where he was burned and his body was not found. John Malalas (*Chronicle* 13.35/343) does not mention the battle of Adrianople in his account of Valens' death – a lacuna occurs at just the wrong moment – but does (perhaps) add to our understanding, stating that Valens was burned in a house and died with his *cubiculari* and *spatharii*. The *cubiculari* were his household staff and the *spatharii* were his bodyguards – the terminology is new, but the sense corroborates the accounts given in other sources.

The most sympathetic account of the battle seems to come from another pagan author, the orator Libanius (*Oration 24*: 3–5). The context of this sympathy was, however, a public oration in which Libanius showed off his rhetorical skill, so we can perhaps take his views with a pinch of salt. The speech was delivered in the presence of the new emperor, Theodosius I, in 379. Libanius states that some people accuse the generals or the soldiers of not being properly trained, or of being cowards; Themistius (*Oration 15*: 189d) accuses the soldiers of cowardice and Valens' generals of indifference, but Libanius will have none of it. He tells us that they fought and died in their ranks, staining the ground of Thrace with their blood, and that the soldiers, commanders and the emperor himself fell together. Libanius' account of Valens' death is different, too; he tells us that Valens was offered a horse upon which to escape, but refused it, saying it was wrong to live on after so many had died. Libanius states that the Romans' morale, training and skill were the same as those qualities of their forebears, as was their love of glory; they fought amid heat and thirst against sword and flame, and preferred death to flight. Libanius also says that some supernatural being must have fought on the side of the 'barbarians' to defeat such an army as this.

Rhetorical hyperbole aside, Libanius mentions flame as playing a part in the battle, and seems to suggest the size of the Roman forces. Ammianus mentions the fires in passing (31.12.13, 31.13.1 & 31.13.8) and no modern reconstruction has bothered much about them. Themistius (*Oration 16*: 206d–207a) also makes a flame analogy when referring to the battle, so this theme must have been present in contemporary minds as part of the battle itself. It might be argued that this flame idea arose from stories about Valens burning to death, and the Christian authors who saw such a fate as divine retribution. Alternatively, it may allude to wider depravations committed by the Goths, but, as we have seen, fire may have played an important part in the Gothic battle plan. What is more, Ammianus, Libanius and Themistius were all pagan and can hardly be argued to have adopted Christian imagery.

Analysis

ROMAN EFFECTIVENESS

The Roman Army which encountered the Goths in 376 had fought the Goths before. There had been campaigns north of the Danube and even Gothic invasions during the 3rd and 4th centuries. The style of warfare the Romans encountered facing the Goths in 376 and after was no different from what they had witnessed before. What was different this time was the scale. In 376, whole peoples crossed into the empire. The situation was exacerbated by the mistreatment of the new arrivals to such an extent that it spurred them to revolt. Our sources mention Gothic oath-breaking, but the Goths' hands were forced by Roman mistreatment.

Roman weapons and armour, and the Roman way of waging war, were not defective. We can tell this by the fact that Goths armed themselves with Roman equipment. Roman swords, armour, shields, helmets and other items of equipment (even axes) were used interchangeably by both sides. Gothic archery was recognized as bringing something of an advance to Roman arms (Vegetius, 1.20) and this may have been in the quantity of archers deployed. Roman logistics were good; the Roman arms factories were operating efficiently – and were targeted by the Goths in an effort to gain more equipment.

What the Romans did not have were sufficient numbers to deal with the numbers of Goths who were in revolt – manpower shortages that seem to have been something Valens recognized. Some authors, such as Ammianus (31.4.6), blame the fact that the Goths were allowed to enter the empire at all for all Rome's subsequent woes. We see in other sources, however, the acknowledgement that the Goths may well have crossed anyway. Moreover, it was undeniable that the Goths offered a possible solution to Rome's military manpower shortages – whole peoples willing to provide frontier armies to protect the empire. Even after the battle of Adrianople, Theodosius I would

This *nummus* (a low-value copper coin) of Theodosius I shows the emperor wearing a ridge helmet and carrying a stylized miniature spear and shield. (York Museums Trust/ Wikimedia/CC BY-SA 4.0)

Dating from *c.*390, the Obelisk of Theodosius is located in the Hippodrome of Constantinople (modern-day Istanbul, Turkey). In this detail from the north face of the Obelisk, the emperor is depicted amid ranks of soldiers. Damage has obscured the holder of the Chi Rho *labarum*, the standard carried by the Christian *legiones* in the battles of the 4th century. (Roweromaniak/Wikimedia/CC BY-SA 2.5)

recruit an army from the Goths still living north of the Danube, with disastrous consequences – they deserted to the enemy – demonstrating that the Romans did not learn their lesson definitively in 378.

Another defect in the Roman attitude towards the Goths – especially in 376, 377 and 378 – was complacency, something contemporaries recognized. Vegetius, who may have written as early as 383, may refer specifically to the battle of Adrianople when he counsels against fighting a pitched battle after a long march (3.11 and also 3.3 & 3.10) and urges his Roman readers to gauge the enemy's strength (3.9 and 3.26), advice Valens and his generals would have done well to have heeded. Vegetius offered several reforms to the Roman military system that recognized these defects in several areas. Vegetius blames Roman defeats on a lack of training and discipline, but this seems not to have been the case – as was demonstrated at the Willows and even at Adrianople, where Roman troops successfully withstood Gothic attacks until the evening came on.

Other writers blamed Valens for allowing laxity in recruitment to creep in, but such issues had been present before his reign. In 376 there seems to have been a sense among the Romans that the Goths were a defeated people, largely disarmed, and could be treated with disdain and exploited with impunity. This led to the atrocities initiated by Lupicinus and Maximus and perpetrated by their troops. Valens had directed his men to treat these new entrants to the empire appropriately, but such orders were ignored by the men on the ground. When Gothic anger erupted, the Romans were unprepared for the consequences.

The Romans also seriously underestimated their Gothic enemies once they were roused, both in terms of capability and, despite contemporary ideas that they were 'tricky' and not to be trusted, that they could be employing stratagems and display tactical know-how. The stereotype presented in the sources is that the Goths were a rampaging horde incapable of employing strategy. At several points the Romans seem to have suffered from a failure of imagination and were consequently forced to react to Gothic initiatives; in some cases the Romans were successful in doing so, in others they were not.

This raises the issues of Roman command. Valens has received most of the blame for insisting on fighting at the battle of Adrianople, and for insisting on fighting alone without waiting for Gratian. Yet as a group, the commanders of Rome's armies in 376–78, for the most part, proved ineffective or were undermined. Richomeres, Sebastianus and Frigiderius had some success, but none of the others did. Sebastianus was undermined (or may have exaggerated his successes), Richomeres had only partial success (if we consider the battle of the Willows to have been a draw) and Frigiderius won against an isolated band, but all the other Roman commanders we find named, including Valens, seem to have underestimated the Goths and paid dearly for it. Julius (the *magister militum* at Constantinople) proved to be an effective commander immediately after the defeat at Adrianople and Richomeres would go on to greater commands, so good leaders were available to the Romans, but many were not utilized or listened to when they were most needed.

This detail from the west face of the base of the Obelisk of Theodosius shows soldiers arrayed next to the emperor. The soldiers' long hair is readily apparent (marking them as Goths). (Gryffindor/ Wikimedia/Public Domain)

GOTHIC EFFECTIVENESS

In their early encounters with the Romans in 376 and 377, two key assets the Goths demonstrated were ferocity and desperation, exhibited on a scale unexpected by their Roman enemies, who believed them to be cowed and beaten. Even without weapons, the Goths were able to overwhelm better-armed and presumably better-trained opponents. Even at the Willows the Goths charged a prepared enemy and seem to have overwhelmed them with the unexpected ferocity of their attack. They also had superiority in numbers, all of whom were raised in a warrior culture designed to create men who were willing to perform brave deeds in front of their chief to earn respect and rewards. They were therefore formidable and willing to fight with whatever weapons came to hand.

The degree to which the Goths were disarmed when they crossed the Danube in 376 will never truly be known. In many cases, the sources argue that the Goths were intending to break their oaths and so brought weapons across with them. This attitude tends to spring from the ancient authors not being able to believe that unarmed 'barbarians' could defeat armed Roman soldiers. The sources seem not to have taken into account just how mistreated, desperate and determined the Goths were. Brought up in a culture which lauded brave deeds, they were willing to throw themselves at their armed guards with enough determination to overwhelm their captors – and thereby arm themselves. Even after Marcianopolis, we find stories of Goths arming themselves with Roman equipment, so there must still have been unarmed warriors in their ranks. The equipment they appropriated was not unfamiliar and so we see that Roman weapons, armour, shields and helmets were interchangeable with their own. They must, therefore, have trained in the

A detail from the south face of the Obelisk of Theodosius. Torcs and long hair mark these men out as Gothic warriors in the emperor's service. (G.dalorto/ Wikimedia/CC BY-SA 2.5)

use of such weapons even though we have no evidence of what that training might have been.

It would be wrong, however, to assume that the Goths were just a horde. We do find some sources emphasizing their ravaging of the countryside, but there are clues that the Goths' activities were more complex. They used deserters to great effect and even false reports – Sebastianus being refused entry to Adrianople being but one example. While it is true that the impetus of the charge was the Goths' principal battle tactic, it is possible to discern – especially at Adrianople – much more depth to their tactical thinking. At the Willows they sought the high ground from which to charge and this may have been part of the cavalry's position at Adrianople. They used a vast number of archers too, so Gothic warfare was not simply a matter of charging headlong at the enemy. Moreover, the appearance from within the wagon laager of the unexpected Gothic contingent at Adrianople shows that they could use their reserves effectively. This may even have been a measure the Goths observed the Romans employ with such good effect at the Willows and copied at Adrianople. The Gothic cavalry onslaught at Adrianople also shows that they could deliver precisely timed tactical charges. The idea that the fires at Adrianople were a smoke signal adds yet another layer to this tactical complexity.

Gothic warriors made good soldiers. They had been employed in Roman armies before 376 and after Adrianople they would be used in ever increasing numbers. Despite Vegetius' warning (1.2) that men from the north did not make good recruits, this was not borne out by the sheer number of Goths who served in Rome's armies. Goths in the service of Rome came with their own problems, however. They remained Arian Christians, which put them at odds with most of their (Nicene Christian) employers; they also continued to hold true to loyalties to their own leaders (as Alaric would show) and so could always be coaxed away from loyalty to Rome – even though some examples, such as Stilicho, a Vandal who came to supreme power in the 390s, would provide a counter to this argument.

Many of the tricks and plans of the Goths during 376–78 should be credited to Fritigern's leadership. The sources (especially Ammianus and Jordanes) tell us of his cunning and knowledge of waging war, although without crediting an actual trick to him, perhaps with the exception of his bluff at Marcianopolis. His leadership can also be seen as being remarkably secure. Alatheus and Saphrax seem to have deferred to him and, at the very least, to have gone along with his plans, as do the leaders of the other Gothic contingents. If Adrianople involved a delayed Gothic charge and also the deliberate baiting of the Romans to provoke an attack, then Fritigern's tactical abilities have been seriously underestimated. He was also able to think strategically and the withdrawals of the Goths – not only away from the walls of Marcianopolis, Adrianople and Constantinople, but also to the Haemus and Rhodope mountains to avoid fighting – show a degree of strategic acumen unacknowledged by his Roman contemporaries. In this unified (and able) leadership the Goths had an advantage over the Romans they opposed. Fritigern offered a unified vision at a time when the Romans were plagued with commanders influenced by court intrigues or who were corrupt and, for the most part, incompetent.

Aftermath

Immediately after their crushing victory over Valens and his men, the Goths made their way to Adrianople, intending to take the city itself, which contained the imperial treasury (Ammianus, 31.15.2). They surrounded the city, but still lacked siege equipment and ignored Fritigern's advice to avoid making war against stone walls. The Roman troops in the city – those who had survived the battle and made it back, and those who guarded the treasury – put up a stout and determined resistance. Ammianus tells (31.15.4) of a unit of 300 soldiers who formed a *cuneus*, but were butchered to a man by ferocious Goths mad with blood-lust. The weather closed in and the Goths returned to their wagon laager, sending a letter demanding that the city surrender. They then attempted to take Adrianople by stratagem – using false deserters to set fire to the city (Ammianus, 31.15.8–9) – but it was successfully defended. The Goths moved on to attempt to take Perinthus and Constantinople, but were no more effective.

These campaigns suggest that the whole of Thrace may have been denuded of Roman troops except for those in the cities. Constantinople was successfully defended by Julius, the *magister militum* of the East – who had not been at Adrianople – or, according to Socrates (5.1.3) and Sozomen (7.1.2), by Valens' wife, the empress Dominica (r. 364–78). Julius also lured other Goths who had been living within the empire to the suburbs of Constantinople and had them massacred (Ammianus, 31.16.8). The revolt had spread; Goths in Pontus and elsewhere revolted too and across the empire, from Milan to Antioch, there was immense worry among the Romans as to what the defeat at Adrianople foretold.

The new emperor, Theodosius I, a Spaniard and successful general, was appointed in late January 379. By this time the East had been without an emperor for almost six months; Valens had died childless. Theodosius had been a successful *dux Moesiae* in the early 370s, but had retired to Spain. He now returned to active service (he may have been recalled as *dux* immediately

This ivory diptych in Monza Cathedral, Italy, dates from the late 4th century and may represent Stilicho, the general who served Theodosius I and Honorius (r. 393–423), or the Roman general Aetius. Stilicho joined the Roman Army and rose through the ranks to the highest position, becoming *magister militum* and then regent for the underage Honorius. Probably born in the early 360s, Stilicho did not serve in the wars of the 370s. (Archiv Gerstenberg/ullstein bild via Getty Images)

The road through the Golden Gate of Constantinople led to the city of Adrianople and the Goths would have headed along it to besiege Constantinople after their victory at Adrianople in 378. The substantial walls of Constantinople withstood a siege mounted by the Goths in 378 and were strengthened under Theodosius II (r. 402–50) in approximately 413. (Frédéric Soltan/Corbis via Getty Images)

after Adrianople), initially basing himself at Thessaloniki in Greece as he could not reach Constantinople. Our sources make mention of Theodosius I's restoration of military discipline. This is peculiar, as within two years he had raised an army (with many Goths in it) which went on to desert him; he then paid off the Goths in exchange for a promise of peace. The pro-Theodosian picture springs, therefore, not from anything new that Theodosius I did, but from the fact that he espoused the orthodox Nicene faith (indeed, this was probably one of the reasons for his appointment). This very obvious bias in the sources makes it difficult to use them, especially when all Roman faults are blamed on Valens' Arianism. A pro-Theodosian stance was obviously about more than faith, as Jordanes and others admit that down to their own time the Goths remained adherents of Arianism.

Gratian recognized Theodosius I, but soon left to return to the West and would offer the new Eastern Roman Emperor little assistance. Theodosius I set about recruiting a new army. Men were conscripted and Goths and other non-Romans were recruited from beyond the Danube. One of the major criticisms advanced by Vegetius throughout Book 1 of his *Epitoma rei militaris* concerned the recruitment of too many 'barbarians' into the armies (see also 2.3 and 2.18). Much of this new army melted away or joined the Goths under Fritigern, although the Goths were pushed back into Thrace from Illyricum and Pannonia and also from Thessaly and Macedonia to where they had spread in 380 and 381. Peace was made in 382: the Goths were incorporated into the empire, and thereafter vast numbers of them were recruited into Roman armies, as the archaeological record attests. The Goths were given lands within Thrace, mainly in Moesia Secunda and Scythia, and granted the status of *foederati* (allies). Settling Goths within the empire, however, was a hazardous development for the Romans, and in the next generation the Goths under Alaric would revolt in 395 and sack Rome in 410 – the next step in the demise of Rome.

BIBLIOGRAPHY

Sources

At times, the historians of the Goths and the Gothic Wars can seem thin on the ground. We have **Ammianus Marcellinus**, whose work, the *Rerum gestarum libri* (known as the *Res gestae* or just referred to by Ammianus' name and book and chapter number), is our best and most reliable source for the period; it is unfortunate that the earlier part of his history, the first 13 books, is lost. The surviving books of his history pick up in 353 and relate Roman history down to the immediate aftermath of the battle of Adrianople, with which he concludes his history in book 31. Ammianus had himself been a soldier, born to a wealthy Greek family in Syrian Antioch around 330. Antioch was then one of the most important cities in the Roman world, with a flourishing intellectual culture of its own. Ammianus was a member of the *protectores domestici* of Constantius II. In 353 Ammianus was attached to the staff of Ursinicus, with whom he campaigned in Gaul, Pannonia and Persia. Ammianus was an eyewitness to the siege of Amida in 359 (19.1–7) and participated in Julian's Persian campaign in 363 (23.5.7, for which he uses the first person). After Julian's death and the Roman retreat from Persia, Ammianus remained in Antioch, although he travelled to Egypt in 366. His military career was perhaps 15 years long; he is a rarity among ancient historians for having actually been a soldier. Some surviving works were written by men in command, but most were written by what we would call 'armchair' historians, so Ammianus' insights are invaluable. Ammianus probably researched and read at Antioch for his history and must have maintained his contacts in the Roman Army as sources for his information after he left service. After the death of Valens in 378, Ammianus travelled to Rome by land and took the time to inspect the battlefields of the recent wars on his way (31.7.16). He continued to write his history in Rome and died sometime after 391, the date of the latest event he refers to (26.5.14).

Ammianus was not a Christian but a traditional Hellenist, a pagan, an adherence still common even in the late 4th century although it makes him unusual among our surviving sources. Other useful pagan authors include the orator **Libanius** (also from Antioch) and **Eunapius** (from Sardis), who explore the Gothic Wars in different ways. Eunapius' *Historia he meta Dexippon* (*Chronicle after Dexippus*) – known as the *Universal History* – is lost, but doubtless dealt with the wars in more detail; some sections of **Zosimus**' *Nea historia* (*New History*) from the late 5th and early 6th centuries incorporated Eunapius' work.

Many of our other sources are Christian, and they frame the history of the wars in those terms – especially as Valens was an Arian Christian, a sect condemned as heretical by orthodox Nicene Christians (Arians believed that the Father was more important than the Son in the Holy Trinity). Thus, these writers saw Valens as justly punished for his heresy at the battle of Adrianople (especially those versions of his demise in which he was burned alive) and the Goths, who converted to Arianism, as being misled. These authors can still offer insights which are useful and sometimes add to what we know from Ammianus (occasionally disagreeing with him). One such is **Jordanes**, a Goth himself who wrote a history of the Goths, *De origine actibusque Getarum* (*The Origin and Deeds of the Goths*), known as the *Getica*, in the 6th century; his account contains information to which Ammianus did not have access, even though Jordanes' account of the wars is relatively brief. **Orosius**, a priest, was born in the 370s (perhaps in Bracara Augusta (modern-day Braga, Portugal) and worked with Augustine of Hippo, dying in 418. Orosius wrote *Historiarum adversum Paganos Libri VII* (*Seven Books of History against the Pagans*), a work that includes an analysis of some aspects of the Gothic Wars. **Sozomen**, writing in the first half of the 5th century, wrote *Historia ecclesiastica* (*Ecclesiastical History*) which also includes useful

This fresco from the Dura-Europos synagogue, North Wall B Register, depicts the battle of Eben-Ezer in the Book of Samuel but shows arms and armour of the mid-3rd century. We see various armours, swords and shields that correspond to types dating from the 3rd and 4th centuries and beyond. Several of the soldiers seem to be bareheaded. The synagogue was adjacent to the wall of the fort (near Tower 17) when it was besieged. (Marsyas/Wikimedia/Public Domain)

information, as do his contemporaries **Socrates of Constantinople**, **Philostorgius** and **Theodoret**, who all wrote *Ecclesiastical Histories*. Often, a single phrase in one of these works can provide an insight absent from our other sources. One such example is Sozomen's 'secure location' (6.40) – on a hill – for the Gothic wagon laager at the battle of Adrianople, or Libanius' idea of the Romans fighting through fire. This flame idea is repeated by the orator **Themistius**.

Various letters such as those of the Roman politician **Symmachus**, **Eusebius of Samosata** and **Basil, bishop of Caesarea**, can be useful, as can the *Fasti Consulares*, the official chronicles attached to editions of the *Chronicle* of **Hydatius**, the 5th-century bishop of Aquae Flaviae (perhaps modern-day Chaves, Portugal). Chronicles themselves, especially the *Chronicon* of **Jerome** and the ***Consularia Constantinopolitana***, are also useful.

Unfortunately, the tradition of inscriptions on military tombstones died out in the 3rd and 4th centuries, leaving large gaps in our knowledge. We can, however, use the ***Codex Theodosianus***, a law code compiled in 438, for military laws which provide insights into Roman Army organization that are absent from the histories and the archaeological record. There are also a plethora of references to the Gothic Wars that tell us little (except about the sense of shock and the magnitude of the loss following the battle of Adrianople) from all manner of surviving accounts from the late 4th century, which have been mentioned only when relevant.

Ancient works

Agathias, 'The Histories', trans. J.D. Frendo (1975), in *Corpus Fontium Historiae Byzantinae* vol. 2A, Series Berolinensis. Berlin: Walter de Gruyter.

Ammianus Marcellinus, *Rerum gestarum libri*, trans. C.D. Yonge (1862). London: Henry. G. Bohn.

Eunapius, *Historia* (Fragments), trans. R.C. Blockley (1983), in *The Fragmentary Classicising Historians of the Later Roman Empire*. Cambridge: Francis Cairns.

Eunapius, *Lives of the Sophists*, trans. W.C. Wright (1921). Cambridge, MA & London: Harvard University Press.

Hydatius, *The Chronicle of Hydatius and the Consularia Constantinopolitana*, trans. R.W. Burgess (1993). Oxford: Clarendon Press.

Jerome, *Chronicon*, trans. M.D. Donaldson (1996). *A Translation of Jerome's Chronicon with Historical Commentary*. Lewiston, NY: Mellen University Press.

John Malalas, *Chronicle*, trans. E. Jeffreys, M. Jeffreys & R. Scott (1986). Melbourne: Australian Association for Byzantine Studies.

Jordanes, *The Gothic History*, trans. C.C. Mierow (1915). Princeton, NJ: Princeton University Press.

Libanius, *Selected Works*, trans. A.F. Norman (1969). Three volumes (Vol. 1, *Oration 24*). Cambridge, MA & London: Harvard University Press.

Orosius, *Seven Books of History against the Pagans*, trans. A.T. Fear (2010). Liverpool: Liverpool University Press.

Philostorgius, *Church History*, trans. P.R. Amidon (2007). Atlanta, GA: Society of Biblical Literature.

Socrates, 'Ecclesiastical History', trans. A.C. Zenos (1890), in P. Schaff and H. Wace, eds, *Nicene and Post-Nicene Fathers*, Second Series, Vol. 2. Buffalo, NY: Christian Literature Publishing Co.

Sozomen, *Ecclesiastical History*, trans. E. Walford (1855). London: Henry G. Bohn.

Themistius, *Orations*, trans. P.J. Heather & D. Moncur (2001). *Politics, philosophy, and empire in the fourth century: select orations of Themistius* (*Oration 16*). Liverpool: Liverpool University Press.

Theodoret, 'Ecclesiastical History', trans. B. Jackson (1892), in P. Schaff and H. Wace, eds, *Nicene and Post-Nicene Fathers*, Second Series, Vol. 3. Buffalo, NY: Christian Literature Publishing Co.

Vegetius, *Epitome of Military Science*, trans. N.P. Milner (1993). Liverpool: Liverpool University Press.

Zosimus, *New History*, trans. R.T. Ridley (1982). Canberra: Australian Association for Byzantine Studies.

Modern works

Austin, N.J.E. (1972). 'Ammianus' Account of the Adrianople Campaign: Some Strategic Observations', *Acta Classica* 15: 77–83.

Austin, N.J.E. (1979). *Ammianus on Warfare. An investigation into Ammianus' military knowledge*. Brussels: Collection Latomus.

Burns, T.S. (1973). 'The battle of Adrianople: a reconsideration', *Historia* 22: 336–45.

Coombs-Hoar, A. (2015). *Eagles in the Dust: The Roman Defeat at Adrianople*. Barnsley: Pen & Sword.

Crump, G. (1975). *Ammianus Marcellinus as a Military Historian*. Historia Zeitschrift für alte Geschichte: Einzelschriften, Heft 27. Wiesbaden: Franz Steiner Verlag.

Delbrück, H., trans. Walter J. Renfroe, Jr. (1980). *The Barbarian Invasions* (*History of the Art of War Vol. II*). Lincoln, NE: University of Nebraska Press. Originally published in German in 1921.

Donnelly, P. (2013). 'What Happened at Adrianople. A re-examination of the campaign and battle of Adrianople, August 378 CE'. Available at http://skookumpete.com/adrianople.htm (last updated November 2019).

Elton, H. (1996). *Warfare in Roman Europe AD 350–425*. Oxford: Oxford University Press.

Gibbon, E. (1776). *The History of the Decline and Fall of the Roman Empire*. Volume 1. London: W. Strahan & T. Cadell.

Gibbon, E. (1781). *The History of the Decline and Fall of the Roman Empire*. Volume 2. London: W. Strahan & T. Cadell.

Heather, P. (1991). *Goths and Romans 332–489*. Oxford: Clarendon Press.

Heather, P. (1996). *The Goths*. Oxford: Blackwell Publishers.

Heather, P. & Matthews, J. (1991). *The Goths in the Fourth Century*. Liverpool: Liverpool University Press.

Hughes, I. (2013). *Imperial Brothers: Valentinian, Valens and the Disaster at Adrianople*. Barnsley: Pen & Sword.

Jones, A.H.M. (1964). *The Later Roman Empire 284–602*. Two volumes. Norman, OK: University of Oklahoma Press.

Lenski, N. (1997). '*Initium mali Romano imperio*: Contemporary Reactions to the Battle of Adrianople', *Transactions and Proceedings of the American Philological Association* 127: 129–68.

Lenski, N. (2002). *Failure of Empire: Valens and the Roman State in the Fourth Century A.D.* Berkeley, CA: University of California Press.

Matthews, J. (2007). *The Roman Empire of Ammianus*. Revised edition. Ann Arbor, MI: Michigan Classical Press.

MacDowall, S. (2001). *Adrianople AD 378: The Goths crush Rome's legions*. Campaign 84. Oxford: Osprey Publishing.

Nicasie, M.J. (1998). *Twilight of Empire: The Roman Army from the Reign of Diocletian until the Battle of Adrianople*. Amsterdam: J.C. Gieben.

Southern, P. & Dixon, K.R. (1996). *The Late Roman Army*. New Haven, CT: Yale University Press.

Thompson, E.A. (1947). *The Historical Work of Ammianus Marcellinus*. Cambridge: Cambridge University Press.

Wolfram, H., trans. T.J. Dunlap (2005). *The Roman Empire and its Germanic Peoples*. Berkeley & Los Angeles, CA: University of California Press. Originally published in German in 1990.

INDEX

References to illustrations are shown in **bold**. References to plates are shown in bold with caption pages in brackets, e.g. **46–47**, (48).